3

636.8089 CAN

Caring ... ey disease

by Dr Sarah Cane

Published by Cat Professional

Copyright © Cat Professional 2012

www.catprofessional.com

ISBN 978-1-908583-01-7

About Cat Professional

Cat Professional is a subdivision of Vet Professionals Ltd. Cat Professional was founded in 2007 by Dr Sarah Caney with the aims of providing cat owners and veterinary professionals with the highest quality information, advice, training and consultancy services.

Publications

Cat Professional is a leading provider of high quality publications on caring for cats with a variety of medical conditions. Written by international experts in their field, each book is written to be understood by cat owners and veterinary professionals. The books are available to buy through the website www.catprofessional.com as eBooks where they can be downloaded and read instantly. Alternatively, they can be purchased as a softback via the website and good bookstores.

'Caring for a cat with kidney disease' was first published (as 'Caring for a cat with kidney failure') in January 2008. This updated edition was published in June 2012. Other books in the Cat Professional series include:

- 'Caring for a blind cat' by Natasha Mitchell

- 'Caring for a cat with hyperthyroidism' by Dr Sarah Caney

- 'Caring for a cat with lower urinary tract disease' by Dr Sarah Caney and Professor Danièlle Gunn-Moore.

- 'Caring for an overweight cat' by Andrea Harvey and Samantha Taylor

A variety of free-to-download articles and videos also feature on the Cat Professional website.

Advice, Training and Consultancy

Cat Professional is dedicated to improving the standards of cat care and in this capacity is a provider of Continuing Professional Development to veterinarians, veterinary nurses and other professionals working with cats around the world.

Cat Professional also works closely with leading providers of cat products and foods providing training programmes, assisting with product literature and advising on product design and marketing.

Specialist feline medicine advice is available to veterinary professionals and cat owners world-wide. Details are available on the website.

About the author

Sarah (pictured right) is an internationally recognised veterinary specialist in feline medicine who has worked as a feline-only vet since 1994. She trained as a specialist at the University of Bristol, England and is one of only fourteen recognised specialists in feline medicine working within the UK. Sarah has written many articles for veterinarians and cat owners and works very closely with the UK cat charity, the Feline Advisory Bureau, FAB (www.fabcats.org). Sarah has written two other books pubished by Cat Professional – 'Caring for a cat with hyperthyroidism' and 'Caring for a cat with lower urinary tract disease' (the latter co-authored with Professor Danièlle Gunn-Moore). As a clinician she enjoys seeing a mixture of first opinion and referral feline patients. She has been invited to lecture on feline medicine at veterinary conferences all over the world.

The cat pictured below right is Hobi, Sarah's very special elderly cat . Sadly Hobi died as a result of various medical problems – including chronic kidney disease – in April 2011.

About this book

This book has been written as both a printed book and an interactive electronic book.

Words in colour are contained in the glossary section at the end of the book.

Dedications and acknowledgements

Thanks go to all of those colleagues, clients and friends for their advice on what should be included.

The pictures included in this book are the copyright of the author except for the two of Morgan at home, kindly included with the permission of her owner.

The author would like to dedicate this edition to the memory of Morgan, the inspiring patient described on pages 51-54 who died on 24th January 2012.

CONTENTS

Chronic kidney disease (CKD) is one of the most common diagnoses made in veterinary practice. Over the last ten years there have been an enormous number of advances both in our understanding of CKD and in our success in treating it. Of all of the treatments available, most proven to benefit cats with CKD is feeding a special kidney prescription diet. Renal prescription diets are modified in many ways to help support cats with CKD. CKD patients fed a renal prescription diet live, on average, more than twice as long as those CKD patients fed standard cat food and their quality of life is improved throughout this time. One important modification of renal diets is that these contain low levels of phosphate. Use of renal prescription diets and/or intestinal phosphate binders which reduce the amount of phosphate absorbed through the bowel is known to benefit affected cats by helping to prevent hyperphosphataemia (increased blood phosphate levels). Hyperphosphataemia is common in patients with CKD and is an important contributor both to clinical signs of ill health and shortened lifespan. It is also vital to ensure that cats with CKD do not become dehydrated, a common complication of this illness, as this worsens their kidney function as well as making them feel unwell. Care providers can help to prevent dehydration in a number of ways, as detailed later in this book. A large number of other treatments such as medication to reduce blood pressure, appetite enhancers and anti-sickness drugs can also have a huge impact on the quality of life of affected cats.

In the long-term, a good relationship between care provider and veterinary practice is essential to provide the best quality and length of life possible. Check-ups are vital to ensure that new complications of CKD are identified and treated as quickly as possible. Thanks to better treatment options, it is not unusual for CKD patients to live for several years with a good quality of life following diagnosis. Cats like Morgan, the case report featured in this book, are an inspiration to all!

Our challenge for the future will be to diagnose CKD at an earlier stage such that beneficial treatments can be instituted promptly. Cats are very adept at hiding signs of illness, and clinical signs of CKD are often not apparent until relatively late in the progression of the disease. For this reason, although CKD commonly develops in middle age (cats aged 7 years and above), it is often not diagnosed until the cat is older. 'Well cat' health screening tests are therefore recommended in all cats over the age of 7 years in order to identify this condition as promptly as possible. Urine screening tests offer a quick and easy way of identifying potential cases of CKD although further blood tests are required to confirm the diagnosis. Prompt diagnosis of renal disease allows early therapeutic intervention which aims to extend length of life and improve quality of life.

I hope that you will find this book of help in supporting the care of your cat with CKD.

Dr Sarah Caney

Overall, in the UK, **chronic kidney disease** (CKD) is thought to affect 1% of patients registered to a veterinary practice at any one time. The frequency of CKD is much higher in older cats and is estimated to affect around 30% of cats over the age of 15 years.

This guide has been written to provide cat owners with the information they need to understand this complex condition and provide the best care for their cat. The author regularly lectures on this subject and the contents of this book reflect what she teaches to veterinary students, veterinary nurses, technicians and qualified veterinarians around the world.

Receiving bad news: coping with the emotional side of receiving a diagnosis of kidney disease in your cat

Being told that your cat has kidney disease has probably come as a very nasty shock. You are likely to be on a roller-coaster of emotions with a lot of worry about your cat. This section will aim to reassure you as well as prepare you for what is to come.

My first advice is to stop, take a deep breath and try to remain calm. Take some time to understand and come to terms with the diagnosis and what it means for your cat. Don't rush any decisions. In most cases, all is not lost and there are lots of things that you can do to restore your cat's quality of life. Remember, you are likely to be suffering more than your cat!

What is wrong with my cat/what happens now?

Firstly, a diagnosis of chronic kidney disease (CKD) is not necessarily a death sentence! Although it is a progressive disease, with appropriate care and commitment you can help your cat to live a happy life – often for many years. Even in those severely affected cats needing hospital treatment and intravenous fluids, recovery to a good quality of life is possible. Don't immediately assume that your cat's life is over. However, CKD is a very serious condition– and all cases vary in the level of care that they need. Your veterinarian is in the best position to advise you on your own cat and what the future might hold – discuss your concerns with them. At the worst, if diagnosed in severe CKD, your veterinarian might advise you that euthanasia (putting your cat to sleep) is the kindest option rather than any treatment. Terrible though this is, this is only the case in the minority of cats with kidney disease.

A diagnosis of kidney disease means that your cat's kidneys are not working as effectively as they should be and this is why your cat has been feeling ill. Section 2 covers the scientific aspects of this condition in much greater detail – you can read about the causes of kidney disease, how veterinarians diagnose the condition and how it can best be treated.

> a diagnosis of kidney disease is not necessarily a death sentence

What caused the kidney disease – was it my fault?

Many owners will immediately panic that they could have done more to prevent the illness from developing or that, if only they had taken their cat to the veterinarian sooner, things might be different. Although it is impossible to generalise and I cannot comment on your own cat's circumstances, in my experience:

■ The overwhelming majority of cases of kidney disease are caused by medical conditions which are completely out of an owner's control i.e. your cat is not ill because of something you have done! There are a few very rare exceptions to this – one would include allowing your cat access to a nephrotoxin (a substance which is toxic to the kidneys). Examples of nephrotoxins include antifreeze (ethylene glycol), lilies, grapes and raisins. This is discussed in more detail in Section 2

Lilies are known to be poisonous to cats if eaten

yourself for not realising that your cat is ill – you are not alone! Early diagnosis of kidney disease usually requires proactive steps from an owner and veterinarian – as will be discussed more in the section: Can kidney disease be diagnosed before clinical signs are present?

Is it possible to prevent kidney disease from occurring in my cat?

Unfortunately it is not possible to prevent kidney disease from occurring in the overwhelming majority of patients – the only examples would be to avoid contact with potential nephrotoxins. Nephrotoxins are discussed in more detail in Section 2.

Since kidney disease is most common in older cats, it is advisable to monitor these cats more closely for evidence of kidney disease – this is especially important since cats are very good at hiding illness from us until it is very advanced. Early diagnosis of kidney disease is discussed in more detail in the section: Can kidney disease be diagnosed before clinical signs are present?

What is the treatment for this disease?

Treatment consists of:

1. Treating the cause of the kidney disease (where this can be found) – for example bacterial infections can be treated with antibiotics.

2. Helping the cat to cope with reduced kidney function. Depending on the individual cat and the severity of their disease this includes feeding a special diet, helping the cat to maintain a normal state of hydration (ie prevent dehydration) and using medication that helps to reduce vomiting, improve the appetite and so on.

■ Although it is always advisable to take your cat to the veterinarian as soon as you realise it is ill, in most situations a short delay is unlikely to have changed their chances of recovery. Again there are some exceptions to this but they are rare – for example causes of sudden kidney problems like the example of eating lilies highlighted above. This can be a rapidly deteriorating condition and every second counts when it comes to treatment!

Cats are masters of hiding illness and, in most circumstances, we only realise our cats are ill when things have got really bad. Most of the signs of illness that a cat shows are also vague – such as sleeping more and slowly losing weight. These signs can be very gradual and hard to spot on a day to day basis. Don't punish

Section 2 discusses this in greater detail – the treatment for kidney disease is complicated as normal kidneys perform many vital functions. In the first instance, your veterinarian may suggest that your cat is admitted to their hospital for intravenous fluid therapy (putting your cat on a drip). This is an effective treatment for dehydration which is common in CKD patients and often provides a significant 'boost' to affected cats. In most cases, the cat will not need to stay on a drip for more than a few days after which it can return home for treatment with you.

Is my cat in pain?

Kidney disease certainly makes a cat feel unwell but it is not usually a painful condition for the majority of cats. Exceptions would include some cats with kidney and/or bladder stones. Your veterinarian will be able to advise you whether or not your cat is in any pain or distress and what treatments are available to help this.

Is it fair to put my cat on lots of different medications – am I being cruel to treat it?

Not all cats with kidney disease need medication. Feeding a kidney prescription diet is usually the most important treatment. Further medication beyond this will depend on your cat and whether they need certain drugs. In some cases, cats with kidney disease do need lots of different medicines and the thought of giving these to your cat can be daunting. My advice, would be not to give up without trying therapy as:

- some cats are surprisingly easy to medicate

- some cats will eat treatments reliably in their food

- for those cats on multiple medications empty gelatine capsules obtained from a veterinarian or pharmacist can be very helpful. Several medicines can be put into one empty

gelatine capsule reducing medication into one easy dosage. This was very helpful for Morgan (the case illustrated in Section 3) and has meant that her medication takes only a few seconds every day and does not cause her any suffering or distress.

It may take some time for you, and your cat, to get used to all of the treatments your veterinarian has suggested but as long as your cat is happy and coping, it is worthwhile persevering. Don't forget to discuss how treatment is going with your veterinarian – if you are having problems, they may well have solutions or suggestions for you. If you find that you are having difficulties giving multiple medications to your cat, discuss these with your veterinarian who can advise you on which medications are most important for your cat.

Also, remember that we are talking about your cat – no one knows your cat better than you and if you feel that the treatment suggested is not right, for whatever reason, then your veterinarian should respect this.

I'm not sure I can cope with treating my cat – help!

Learning of a diagnosis of kidney disease is going to come as a shock and will take some time to get used to. Once you have had a chance to think things through, chat with friends/family and your veterinarian, hopefully everything will seem clearer and less daunting.

You can only do your best when it comes to caring for your cat and it is not always possible to do everything you want. For example if you have severe arthritis and are unable to give your cat a pill this may affect the level of treatment you can provide. Likewise, if your cat is completely intolerant to the thought of being medicated, this may prevent you from giving some treatments to it. In many situations, there are other options available – for example trying to hide medications in food or asking your veterinarian to give an injection of the drug. Please note injections are not available for every type of medicine. In any case, your veterinarian should be able to talk you through the options and, together, you should be able to make a plan that you both feel comfortable with.

Is kidney disease life-threatening?

Yes – kidneys are essential body organs so any cat with kidney disease will have a reduced life expectancy. However, many cats with kidney disease can live with an excellent quality of life for several years after the diagnosis is made, especially if they receive treatment for this condition. For example, cats with CKD that will eat a special prescription diet formulated for cats with CKD, have a doubled life expectancy compared to those cats with CKD that will only eat standard cat food. This is discussed in more detail in Section 2.

What is kidney disease?

Kidney disease (also known as kidney failure, kidney insufficiency, renal failure or renal insufficiency) is the term used when kidney function is no longer able to meet the body's demands. The more emotive term 'failure' is used less frequently nowadays since many cats previously described as suffering from this can now be stabilised for prolonged periods (for example years!) with treatment. Kidney disease is a broad term which covers cats in all stages of renal disease – from those that have no health complications through to those with significant problems as a result of their illness.

Cats and humans are born with more kidney tissue than is needed – this is called a functional reserve. This is why healthy adult humans can safely donate a kidney to a friend or relative. It is normal, as a cat ages, for there to be some loss of kidney function.

Clinical signs of kidney disease are not seen until at least two thirds of the functional kidney tissue has been lost. Unfortunately this makes it difficult to diagnose cats in the very early stages of kidney disease.

Kidney disease is sub-divided into acute and chronic kidney disease. In medical terminology, acute means sudden (occurring over a period of less than 24 hours) therefore acute renal failure (ARF, also referred to as acute kidney disease) means a sudden loss of kidney function which can be caused by one or more of the following:

- Reduced blood supply to the kidneys (so called pre-renal ARF). Causes include heart failure, shock (for example following a road traffic accident) and dehydration

- Damage to the kidneys themselves (renal or intrinsic ARF). Causes include poisoning e.g. antifreeze (ethylene glycol); eating lilies, grapes or raisins

- Failure of urine excretion due to a blockage in the urethra (tube from the bladder to the outside) or rupture of the bladder. This is called post-renal ARF.

Although many causes of ARF are fully treatable (and the kidney damage can be fully reversed), if severe and untreated, ARF can progress to chronic kidney disease (CKD). In medical terms, chronic means something which has been present for at least 2 weeks. CKD is considered to be a progressive condition – it will get worse with time – although the speed of progression is variable.

Many cats will be presented to their veterinarians when in 'acute on chronic' kidney disease. This is the situation present when a cat in CKD is presented in an acute crisis. The cat may have been coping, more or less, in CKD for some time but for example becoming dehydrated has precipitated a sudden crisis. Cats in acute on chronic crises often benefit from being admitted to a veterinary hospital and placed on an intravenous drip so that they can be rehydrated.

Chronic kidney disease is considered to be a progressive condition – it will get worse with time – although the speed of progression is variable

What do normal kidneys do?

The kidneys are required for a great number of important functions in the body. Normal cats are born with two kidneys, a right and a left kidney, which are located in the abdomen.

Normal kidneys are vital for good health and have many important functions including:

- Excretion of waste products via the urine. This includes protein breakdown products such as urea and creatinine

- Regulation of normal body water content (hydration balance)

- Regulation of levels of blood salts (e.g. sodium, potassium, calcium and phosphate)

- Regulation of body acidity levels

- Production and activation of a number of hormones and other substances (e.g. erythropoietin – a hormone which stimulates production of red blood cells by the bone marrow)

What causes kidney disease?

The causes of kidney disease can be divided into two main categories:

- Congenital (those present at the time of birth) such as:

  - Polycystic kidney disease. This is an inherited cause of kidney disease which is especially common in Persian and related breeds. Affected cats are born with small cysts (fluid filled structures) in their kidney tissue. As the cat gets older, the cysts enlarge and eventually these compromise kidney function by putting pressure on the normal cells. CKD typically develops once two thirds of the kidney tissue has been lost –this is often when the cat is around 4 years old although it can be considerably later in some cases. Approximately 25-35% of Persians around the world are estimated to be affected by this inherited disease

  - Renal dysplasia (abnormal development of one or both kidneys)

  - Being born with only one kidney

- Acquired conditions i.e. the cat is born with normal kidneys but develops a problem in later life. These include:

  - Bacterial and viral infections

  - Inflammatory conditions

  - Toxin exposure e.g. ingesting antifreeze, lilies, grapes or raisins

– **Trauma** e.g. damage to the kidneys following a car accident

– Cancer e.g. lymphoma (a cancer of white blood cells), adenocarcinoma (a cancer of glandular tissues).

Analysis of a kidney **biopsy** from cats with **CKD** often shows that they have **chronic interstitial nephritis** – this term is used to describe the terminal kidney disease (scarring etc) that occurs irrespective of the initiating cause of the kidney disease. Unfortunately this means that it is not usually possible to determine the cause of the kidney disease once it has progressed to this point and is one reason why kidney biopsies are not commonly recommended (see later section **What other tests are helpful in cats with kidney disease?**).

CKD is usually seen as a consequence of an acquired disease and is most common in middle-aged and older cats. Some breeds of cat are more likely to suffer from kidney disease than others – these include Abyssinian, Maine Coon, Persian and Siamese cats. There is no difference in the frequency of males or females affected by kidney disease.

Can kidney disease be prevented?

Many owners will immediately worry that they could have done more to prevent the illness from developing or that if only they had taken their cat to the veterinarian sooner, things might be different. The overwhelming majority of cases of kidney disease are caused by medical conditions which are completely out of an owner's control. There are a few very rare exceptions to this:

■ Poisonings – for example lilies, grapes, raisins and antifreeze are known **nephrotoxins** (substances known to be harmful

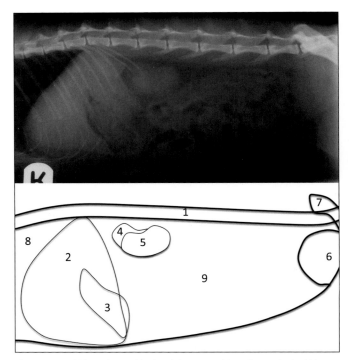

There are two kidneys located in the abdomen. In this **radiograph**, the kidneys are normal in size and are slightly superimposed. Key: 1 – back bone, 2 – liver, 3 – stomach, 4 – right kidney, 5 – left kidney, 6 – bladder, 7 – hip bone, 8 – lung, 9 – bowel loops

to the kidneys) when ingested. Even small quantities of these substances can be fatal if ingested. If you suspect that your cat has been in contact with any of these substances, you should contact your veterinarian immediately. Prompt treatment can be life-saving in some poisoning cases and a complete cure is possible

- Certain drugs – some drugs are known to have the potential to cause kidney damage. Where these are needed in your cat, your veterinarian should discuss the potential for side-effects with you. Examples include certain antibiotics (e.g. gentamicin), non-steroidal anti-inflammatory agents (e.g. meloxicam, carprofen, ketoprofen, robenacoxib). Side-effects can occur with all drugs and all of the drugs listed above can be invaluable in treating cats with a variety of problems. For example, the non-steroidal anti-inflammatory agents provide pain relief and have made an enormous difference to the quality of life of cats with short-term pain (e.g. following a road traffic accident or surgery) and more long-standing conditions (e.g. arthritis). Fortunately in most healthy cats these drugs do not cause any side-effects to the kidneys. Where a cat is known to have kidney disease, your veterinarian may recommend that these drugs are used at a much lower dose or avoided because of the risk of side-effects. Many cats with CKD are able to tolerate non-steroidal anti-inflammatory agents safely when these drugs are used at the lowest effective dose and the cat is closely monitored for problems. As always, your veterinarian is the best person to advise you on the use of these drugs – whether or not your cat has kidney disease.

Although it is always advisable to take your cat to the veterinarian as soon as you realise it is ill, in most situations a short delay is unlikely to have changed their chances of recovery. Again there are some exceptions to this but they are rare – for example cases of acute renal failure.

Therefore, in the majority of cases, there is nothing that can be done to prevent CKD from occurring and, unfortunately, by the time it is obvious that the cat has a problem, at least two thirds of the functional kidney tissue has been irreparably lost. Diagnosis of kidney disease is possible before clinical signs of illness become apparent but it requires proactive testing – this is discussed in more detail in the section Can kidney disease be diagnosed before clinical signs are present?

What are the signs of chronic kidney disease?

The clinical signs of chronic kidney disease vary between individual cats but commonly include (in order of approximate decreasing frequency):

Polydipsia – an excessive thirst – is one of the clinical signs of kidney disease although it can be seen with other medical conditions such as diabetes mellitus ('sugar diabetes').

- Weight loss

- Reduced appetite (inappetence, anorexia)

- Dehydration

- Lethargy – appearing listless and more tired than usual

- Increased thirst (polydipsia)

- Increased urination (polyuria)

- Systemic hypertension (high blood pressure) – this can cause problems with vision (including blindness), collapse, fits, behavioural changes

- Vomiting

- Constipation

- Anaemia (low red blood cell count)

- Mouth ulcers – often associated with bad breath (halitosis).

What is renal secondary hyperparathyroidism?

In healthy cats, the parathyroid glands (small glands located in the neck) help to control blood levels of calcium and phosphate. Cats with CKD are vulnerable to developing a complication called renal secondary hyperparathyroidism where the parathyroid glands enlarge and produce excessive amounts of parathyroid hormone (PTH). Failing kidneys do not produce enough of a hormone called calcitriol (which also helps to control calcium levels) and become less efficient at excreting phosphate in the urine. Increased blood phosphate levels (hyperphosphataemia) and reduced calcitriol levels are the

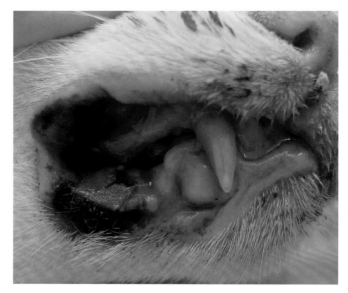

Mouth ulcers can be seen in very sick cats with kidney disease. In this patient, the margins of the lips in the left of the picture are swollen with areas that are greeny-brown in colour. This tissue is dead, infected, very painful and has an unpleasant smell.

main triggers for the development of renal secondary hyperparathyroidism.

Renal secondary hyperparathyroidism is seen in the majority of cats with CKD. Unless treated, renal secondary hyperparathyroidism progressively worsens and is associated with a worse long-term outlook. Cats with renal secondary hyperparathyroidism not only suffer more clinical signs of their renal disease, they are also more likely to die sooner than other CKD cats that do not have this complication. High levels of PTH contribute to the clinical signs of CKD (e.g. poor appetite, vomiting, weight loss) by acting as uraemic toxins, in a similar way to urea and creatinine. High levels of PTH also cause ongoing damage to the kidneys. Long-term consequences of renal secondary hyperparathyroidism include mineral deposits in body tissues (soft tissue mineralization), bone fractures and a condition called 'rubber jaw' where the bones of the jaw become very soft following loss of calcium. Where present, mineralization of the kidneys is especially damaging to renal function.

Renal secondary hyperparathyroidism can be diagnosed by measuring blood levels of parathyroid hormone. This test is often very expensive and requires special sample handling procedures which make it complicated to perform – for example, the sample has to be frozen immediately after collection and transported to the laboratory whilst still frozen. Fortunately, blood phosphate levels, which are much cheaper and easier to measure, are a good indication of parathyroid hormone levels. If blood phosphate levels are high then the cat will have renal secondary hyperparathyroidism; if blood phosphate levels are within the reference range then renal secondary hyperparathyroidism may still be present.

Renal secondary hyperparathyroidism is treated by feeding a phosphate restricted diet and/or using intestinal phosphate binders. Treatment aims to keep blood phosphate levels at the bottom of the reference range such that renal secondary hyperparathyroidism is not triggered. Interpretation of blood phosphate levels in cats with CKD and use of phosphate binders is discussed in more detail on pages 37-38.

How is chronic kidney disease diagnosed?

Diagnosis is made through testing blood and urine samples. In patients with chronic kidney disease, the kidneys will not have been excreting waste efficiently, so the blood will contain higher levels of waste products (such as urea and creatinine). Normal cats and dehydrated cats produce very concentrated (strong) urine – the ability to do this is lost as kidney disease worsens. Thus, cats with CKD have increased blood levels of urea and creatinine (referred to as 'azotaemia') and less concentrated (more dilute) urine. It is essential to test both blood and urine samples since there are other causes of azotaemia (such as dehydration which is common in sick cats) which need to be ruled out. Cats should be fasted for 8 hours before blood is collected since a recent meal can cause a false increase in blood urea levels.

Weight loss is one of the most common findings in a cat with CKD

Urea and creatinine are not perfect measures of renal function since both parameters are affected by other factors – for example:

■ Urea levels can be increased in certain situations including

- Dehydration

- Having eaten recently – for example within a few hours of blood sampling

- Cats that are consuming large amounts of protein – for example cats suffering from hyperthyroidism (an overactive thyroid) are often very hungry and may eat double their normal food intake. Even if fasted before blood sample collection, some of these cats have small increases in their urea levels

■ Urea levels can be decreased in certain situations including

- Cats being fed a low protein diet

- Some cats with liver problems

■ Creatinine levels can be increased in certain situations including:

- Cats with a large amount of muscle – for example, entire male cats (Tom cats)

- Following severe exercise

■ Creatinine levels can be decreased in certain situations including

- Cats in poor muscle condition – for example, very thin cats that have little muscle mass. This is often the case in many elderly cats and can lead to their creatinine levels being lower than expected.

It is common to have a combination of dehydration and CKD in the same patient (sometimes referred to as 'acute on chronic' kidney disease) and this can make the azotaemia even worse – in other words the urea and creatinine levels are higher than is just reflected by the cats kidney disease. If this is the case, then following correction of the dehydration (e.g. intravenous fluids – putting your cat on a drip) the urea and creatinine levels will fall. The level to which they fall is that reflected by the underlying kidney disease therefore the severity of the underlying kidney disease cannot be determined until any dehydration is corrected.

Urine concentration is assessed using a refractometer which measures the urine specific gravity. Water has a specific gravity of 1.000. Normal cats usually produce urine with a specific gravity of at least 1.040. The lower the specific gravity, the more dilute the urine is. Kidney disease reduces a cat's ability to produce concentrated urine and the specific gravity falls to less than 1.035. In severe cases of kidney disease, the urine specific gravity can be as low as 1.015. It is important to bear in mind that other illnesses can affect the specific gravity mimicking CKD – these include:

■ Diabetes mellitus (sugar diabetes): it is common for the urine specific gravity to be between 1.025 and 1.035. Sugar (glucose) is detected in the urine when a 'dipstick' test is done

■ Hyperthyroidism (overactive thyroid): it is common for affected cats to produce slightly dilute urine with a specific gravity of around 1.030

■ Liver disease: some cats with liver disease will produce more dilute urine (lower urine specific gravity)

■ Diabetes insipidus: a rare disease in which affected cats produce very dilute urine (specific gravity less than 1.010).

Different laboratories have different reference ranges for blood test values such as urea and creatinine and, different countries use different units which further confuses matters. The two types of unit measurements used are:

■ Conventional units: mg/dl or mEq/l

■ SI units: most widely used; mmol/l, g/l.

The table below gives a guide to the reference range levels for a number of parameters measured in cats with CKD. N.B. the reference range will vary slightly between laboratories so the following is just a rough guide:

Please note that this is a general guide to reference ranges. IRIS recommends different interpretation of blood phosphate and creatinine levels when considering cats with CKD (as discussed on pages 26-27 and 37-38).

A table with conversion factors for transforming SI units to Conventional units (and vice versa) is contained in the Reference section (Section 5).

Parameter	'Typical reference range' – Conventional units	'Typical reference range' – SI units
Urea	17 – 29 mg/dl	6 – 10.5 mmol/l
Creatinine	< 2 mg/dl	< 175 µmol/l
Phosphate	2.9 – 6.0 mg/dl	0.95 – 1.95 mmol/l
Potassium	4.0 – 5.0 mEq/l	4.00 – 5.00 mmol/l
Sodium	145 – 157 mEq/l	145 – 157 mmol/l
Calcium	8 – 10 mg/dl	2.0 – 2.5 mmol/l
Albumin	2.4 – 3.9 mg/dl	24 – 39 g/l
Globulin	2.5 – 5.5 mg/dl	25 – 55 g/l
Total Protein	5.4 – 7.8 mg/dl	54 – 78 g/l
Bicarbonate	18 – 24 mEq/l	18 – 24 mmol/l
Packed cell volume (PCV) or haematocrit	28 – 45%	0.28 – 0.45
Haemoglobin	0.8 – 1.5 mg/dl	8 – 15 g/l

mg/dl – milligrams per decilitre   µmol/l – micromoles per litre   g/dl – grams per decilitre

mmol/l – millimoles per litre   mEq/l – milliequivalents per litre   g/l – grams per litre.

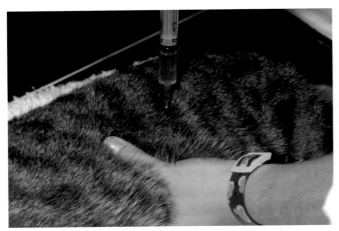

Cystocentesis is a commonly used technique to obtain a urine sample. A needle is passed through the skin and into the bladder from where urine is collected. This is a procedure which is well tolerated by cats and can be done with them fully conscious, gently restrained by a nurse.

'Free catch' urine samples can be collected by using non-absorbent cat litter (Mikki® litter has been placed in this cat's litter tray). Once the cat has urinated the tray is tipped and a syringe or pipette used to collect a sample of urine for analysis.

Collection of blood and urine samples should not be a stressful event for a cat. Blood is most easily collected from the jugular vein which is the largest easily accessible vein and is located in the cat's neck. Alternatively it can be collected from one of the smaller veins such as either a cephalic vein (found on the front surface of the forelimbs) or the saphenous vein (found on the inner surface of the hindlimbs). Urine samples can be collected in a variety of ways:

- Cystocentesis: this is the procedure by which urine is collected using a needle and syringe. The cat is gently held and the needle is passed through the skin of the abdomen into the bladder. This is not a painful procedure and allows collection of a sterile (free from bacterial contamination) sample which is ideal for the tests needed

- Catheter samples: urine can be collected using a catheter which is passed through the urethra (the tube from the outside of the cat to the bladder). Unfortunately this is not an appropriate technique for urine collection in most cats as it requires sedation (providing a state of calm and muscle relaxation using drugs) or anaesthesia (providing a state of unconsciousness, muscle relaxation and loss of pain sensation using certain drugs)

- Free catch samples: urine can be collected from an empty litter tray or one containing non-absorbent cat litter. Lots of different types of non-absorbent cat litter are available from your veterinarian or cheaper alternatives can be used (e.g. clean aquarium gravel, chopped up plastic bags). Once the cat has urinated, the urine can be collected using a syringe or pipette. It is important that the sample is collected as soon as possible after urination. Free catch samples are acceptable for initial assessment of kidney function. For example the refractometer test which determines the concentration of the urine is not affected by the method of collection.

Free catch samples are not suitable for bacterial culture as they will be contaminated by bacteria in the litter tray and on the cat's paws.

Urine should be analysed as quickly as possible although many of the parameters that veterinarians will be most interested in are not critically affected by storage for up to 24 hours. Urine tests include:

- Specific gravity measured using a refractometer

- Urine dipstick to check for sugar (glucose) or other abnormalities

- Sediment examination: looking for cells, bacteria, crystals or other material in the urine sample under a microscope. For example this can help to diagnose a urinary tract infection

- Urine protein tests – for example the urine protein to creatinine ratio (referred to as the UPC or PCR test). This is a laboratory test which quantifies the severity of proteinuria (total amount of protein lost into the urine). Ratios greater than 0.4 are currently considered to be abnormally high in cats with CKD. Cats suffering from proteinuria have a worse long-term outlook than those that do not. Proteinuria can be an indication of renal damage (e.g. more 'leaky' filters in

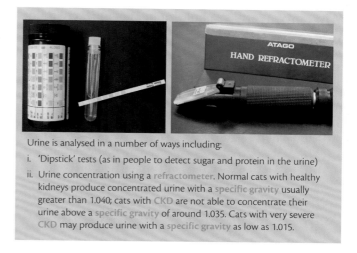

Urine is analysed in a number of ways including:

i. 'Dipstick' tests (as in people to detect sugar and protein in the urine)

ii. Urine concentration using a refractometer. Normal cats with healthy kidneys produce concentrated urine with a specific gravity usually greater than 1.040; cats with CKD are not able to concentrate their urine above a specific gravity of around 1.035. Cats with very severe CKD may produce urine with a specific gravity as low as 1.015.

the glomerulus) but is also known to be damaging to kidney function. Urine dipsticks are not considered to be sufficiently accurate to assess proteinuria in patients. Another protein test your veterinarian may choose would include the microalbuminuria test (a test which measures the amount of a single protein, albumin, in urine). Assessment and treatment of proteinuria is discussed in more detail on pages 26 and 42-43

- Bacterial culture to see whether there is any evidence of infection. When a bacterial infection is diagnosed by the laboratory they will do a sensitivity test to identify which antibiotics are likely to be most effective in treating the infection. This is a test which takes a few days to perform.

What other tests are helpful in cats with chronic kidney disease?

Once a diagnosis has been made, other blood tests (haematology and biochemistry) and urine tests will help to determine whether or not the cat is suffering from any other consequences of their kidney disease. These include:

- Dehydration: blood levels of salts, proteins and red blood cells can help to identify dehydration in affected patients. Dehydration is one of the most common complications of kidney disease, affecting around two thirds of patients. Dehydrated cats will usually be quiet and withdrawn

- Anaemia: low levels of red blood cells can be detected using haematology (also known as a complete blood count, CBC). Anaemic cats will often be quiet and spend more time sleeping or resting than is normal for them. They may demonstrate an abnormal appetite (referred to as 'pica') where they eat cat litter or soil or lick concrete. You may notice that their gums are pale (for example when the cat yawns). Around 30-40% of cats with CKD suffer from anaemia associated with their renal disease

- Altered blood salt levels: most commonly in CKD are increased blood phosphate levels (hyperphosphataemia) and low blood potassium levels (hypokalaemia). Other blood salts which can be affected by CKD include sodium and calcium

  - Cats with hyperphosphataemia may show clinical signs including loss of appetite, vomiting and depression. Hyperphosphataemia is seen in around two thirds of cats with CKD

Cats with CKD are more vulnerable to bacterial urinary tract infections. Affected cats may show clinical signs of cystitis including increased frequency of urination and passing bloody/smelly urine.

– Cats with hypokalaemia may have a poor appetite, be more quiet/withdrawn than normal and in severe cases show dramatic muscle weakness. This can be manifested as an inability to lift the head (see picture on page 38). Around 20-25% of cats with CKD suffer from hypokalaemia

■ Altered blood acidity – acidosis: the blood is more acidic than it should be. Affected cats are often very ill with no appetite and no energy and may vomit. Up to 10% of cats with CKD suffer from severe acidosis requiring specific treatment

■ Proteinuria: In mild to moderate cases, this might not be associated with any specific clinical signs. Cats with more severe or long-standing proteinuria, may develop abnormally low blood protein levels (hypoproteinaemia) which can cause the face, legs and skin of the chest and abdomen to appear puffy or swollen (due to oedema development). Development of fluid in the chest (pleural fluid) or abdomen (ascites) can also be seen and this can cause, respectively, breathlessness and a swollen/enlarged abdomen

■ Bacterial urinary tract infections. Around 20-25% of cats with CKD suffer from bacterial urinary tract infections. Unfortunately, many of these cats do not show specific clinical signs (i.e. the infection is 'silent') and may only show vague clinical signs such as weight loss and lethargy. A small proportion of cats with urinary infections show clinical signs of cystitis including urgency to pass urine, passing small amounts of urine very frequently and passing bloody/smelly urine. Infections of the kidneys (known as pyelonephritis) are usually associated with clinical signs of pain, fever and general malaise. Bacterial urine culture and sensitivity testing is recommended in all CKD patients

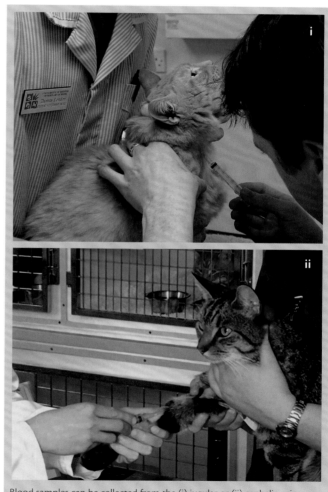

Blood samples can be collected from the (i) jugular or (ii) cephalic veins

■ **Renal secondary hyperparathyroidism.** The majority of cats with CKD suffer from renal secondary hyperparathyroidism which contributes to many of the clinical signs of renal disease. Measurement of parathyroid hormone can be done to diagnose this complication but assessment of blood phosphate levels also provides useful indications of renal secondary hyperparathyroidism. For example. if blood phosphate levels are high then the cat will have renal secondary hyperparathyroidism; if blood phosphate levels are within the reference range then renal secondary hyperparathyroidism may still be present.

It is important to identify and treat any of these additional problems, as it will help to make your cat feel as well as possible. It is also prudent to screen for other concurrent illnesses – it is not unusual to find that cats with CKD have more than one problem!

It is now known that a significant proportion of CKD patients (estimated to be at least 20 per cent) suffer from systemic hypertension (high blood pressure). Systemic hypertension is a serious condition that can result in damage to a number of internal organs. Most at risk, are the so-called 'end organs' which are particularly vulnerable to the damaging effects of high blood pressure. The 'end organs' include the brain, kidney, heart and eyes. In severe cases, untreated systemic hypertension can result in blindness, seizures, heart problems, continued damage to the kidneys, coma and death. Blood pressure can be measured in most practices. If facilities are not available to measure blood pressure, then your veterinarian may refer you to another practice or to a specialist so that this test can be done. Examination of the eyes can be extremely helpful when checking for signs of hypertension – your veterinarian may be able to see abnormalities

Dilation of the pupils (i) is one potential indication of blindness associated with high blood pressure as in this case. When a light is shone into the cat's eyes (ii), the pupils remain large and the retina can be seen (both of these findings are abnormal). Small areas of bleeding can also be seen in the cat's left eye – another consequence of her high blood pressure. Unfortunately the blindness was permanent in this cat.

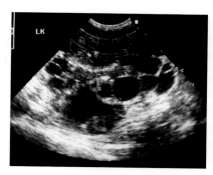

Ultrasound is a very effective way of diagnosing conditions like polycystic kidney disease. In this patient, many black circles corresponding to fluid-filled cysts can be seen on the scan picture of a cat's kidney.

such as bleeding into the eye or retinal detachment (where the retina – the 'seeing' layer of tissue at the back of the eye – lifts off). Systemic hypertension can cause permanent blindness if left untreated.

In some patients, additional tests such as x-rays and ultrasound of the kidneys may be useful for diagnosis. For example, polycystic kidney disease can be diagnosed by ultrasound and many kidney stones will be visible on an x-ray. Ultrasound can usually be performed with the cat fully conscious but x-rays usually require sedation or anaesthesia.

In some cases, it is helpful to collect a kidney biopsy to determine the precise nature of the kidney disease. A biopsy involves collection and laboratory analysis of a sample of tissue such as the kidney. Biopsies can be collected in three main ways:

1. Fine needle aspirate (FNA): the technique by which a sample of cells is aspirated (drawn) out of the kidney using a needle inserted through the skin. This procedure is relatively safe ('non-invasive') but often will not give enough information as to the precise nature of the disease.

2. Needle core biopsy: the technique by which a cylinder of tissue is obtained using a special needle inserted through the skin (under the guidance of ultrasound). This provides more tissue than an FNA but even so may not provide sufficient tissue to always make an accurate diagnosis.

3. Wedge biopsy: the technique by which a wedge of tissue is removed from the kidney via abdominal surgery. This provides the best sample of tissue for a pathologist to examine but involves general anaesthesia (deep sedation can be sufficient for the other two techniques) and the associated surgical and anaesthetic risks.

In general, biopsies are not commonly performed as:

- In most cats with kidney disease, the biopsy results will not affect the treatment that the cat needs

- It is a procedure which carries a high risk of bleeding which can be fatal in some cases

- The procedure requires sedation or anaesthesia which can be risky in some patients with kidney disease

- The biopsy procedure can worsen kidney disease by causing scarring in the kidney

Examples of situations where a biopsy is indicated would include:

- Some cancers e.g. lymphoma – a cancer which responds to drug treatment

- Cats with severe proteinuria

- Young cats with kidney disease

Blood pressure is most accurately measured using a Doppler machine and is a procedure which is very well tolerated by fully conscious cats. A cuff attached to a pressure gauge (called a sphygmomanometer) is placed on a forelimb or the tail; a separate sensor (the Doppler probe) is used to detect the pulse below the cuff. The cuff is inflated until the pulse signal disappears and then deflated slowly. The systolic blood pressure (higher of the two blood pressure readings we get when our own blood pressure is measured) is the pressure at which the pulse is first detectable.

In these situations precise knowledge of the nature of disease can make a difference to the treatment offered and long-term outlook for the affected cat.

What is staging of kidney disease and what does this mean?

The International Renal Interest Society (IRIS: www.iris-kidney. com) has devised a staging system for categorising the severity of stable kidney disease based on laboratory results (blood and urine) and blood pressure. IRIS provides support and advice to veterinarians regarding when to institute different treatments.

Patients are primarily staged according to their blood creatinine levels. It is important to use creatinine values obtained after the cat has been re-hydrated since – as stated earlier – dehydration increases creatinine levels and may give a false impression that the kidney disease is worse than it actually is. Some cats with CKD will pass through all of the IRIS stages as their kidney disease progresses; other cats will remain stable for many years in the same stage. (*see table opposite*)

Substaging according to renal proteinuria

Patients are also staged according to their proteinuria. Most clinicians prefer to use the urine protein to creatinine ratio to assess proteinuria. The proteinuria must be of renal origin – in other words, other causes of proteinuria such as pre-renal (for example some cancers) and post-renal causes (for example urinary tract infections) must be excluded before diagnosing renal proteinuria. Physiological (benign and transient) causes of proteinuria such as exercise, stress and fever should also be excluded as causes. Unless the proteinuria is very severe (UPC > 2.0), it is usually recommended that it is confirmed to be persistent by repeating the test three times over a two week period. UPC results are interpreted in CKD patients as follows:

- Non proteinuric (NP): UPC < 0.2

- Borderline proteinuria (BP): UPC 0.2 – 0.4

- Proteinuric (P): UPC > 0.4. Very high UPC results (> 2.0) are usually indicative of glomerulonephropathies.

IRIS Stage	Description	Plasma creatinine results		Clinical signs?	Comments
		Conventional units	SI units		
1	Non-azotaemic	< 1.6 mg/dl	140 µmol/l	Absent	Patients have some other renal abnormality – for example: • reduced urine concentrating ability (USG < 1.035) without an identifiable non-renal cause • abnormal feeling kidneys on palpation • persistent proteinuria of renal origin • abnormal renal ultrasound • abnormal renal biopsy results • progressively increasing creatinine levels
2	Mild renal azotaemia	1.6 – 2.8 mg/dl	140 – 249 µmol/l	Mild or absent	The lower end of the creatinine range for Stage 2 patients lies within the reference range for many laboratories but is recommended to identify patients suffering from CKD
3	Moderate renal azotaemia	2.9 – 5.0 mg/dl	250 – 439 µmol/l	May be present	
4	Severe renal azotaemia	> 5.0 mg/dl	> 440 µmol/l	Usually present	

Substaging according to systemic blood pressure results

Patients are also staged according to their blood pressure results and whether or not there is evidence of damage associated with the high blood pressure. High blood pressure can occur as a consequence of kidney disease and can damage the kidneys, heart, brain and eyes (see pages 24-25 and 39-40 for more information). IRIS substages patients according to their systolic and diastolic blood pressure readings. The systolic blood pressure is the higher of the two blood pressure readings collected when blood pressure is measured. The substages are:

- Arterial pressure (AP) substage 0: Minimal risk: Systolic blood pressure (SBP) < 150 mmHg; diastolic blood pressure (DBP) < 95 mmHg

- AP substage 1: Low risk: SBP 150-159; DBP 95-99

- AP substage2: Moderate risk: SBP 160-179; DBP 100-119

- AP substage 3: High Risk: SBP ≥180; DBP ≥120.

Patients are further classified according to whether or not they have evidence of end organ damage as a result of their systemic hypertension. Most often, patients with sustained high blood pressure develop problems with their eyesight which can be detected by performing an ocular examination. For example, changes to the size of blood vessels, bleeding into the eye or retinal detachment (where the retina – the 'seeing' layer of tissue

at the back of the eye – lifts off). In those cases where blood pressure measurement has not been possible, a category of risk not determined (RND) is recorded.

Since stress commonly causes a temporary increase in blood pressure (so called 'white coat hypertension'), it is vital that blood pressure is measured in a calm and relaxed manner. In those cats where there is no evidence of end organ damage in spite of high blood pressure readings, a decision might be made to monitor rather than treat the patient in case stress is the cause of the high readings. Treatment of systemic hypertension is discussed in more detail on pages 39-40.

Treatment can make an enormous difference to the cat's quality and length of life

Life stage	Age of cat	Human equivalent
Kitten: birth to 6 months	0 – 1 month	0 – 1 year
	2 – 3 months	2 – 4 years
	4 months	6 – 8 years
	6 months	10 years
Junior: 7 months to 2 years	7 months	12 years
	12 months	15 years
	18 months	21 years
	2 years	24 years
Prime: 3 years to 6 years	3	28
	4	32
	5	36
	6	40
Mature: 7 years to 10 years	7	44
	8	48
	9	52
	10	56
Senior: 11 years to 14 years	11	60
	12	64
	13	68
	14	72
Geriatric: 15 years+	15	76
	16	80
	17	84
	18	88
	19	92
	20	96
	21	100
	22	104
	23	108
	24	112
	25	116

Can kidney disease be diagnosed before clinical signs are present?

Whilst CKD is most common in older cats, it is believed to begin in middle-age. Cats in the early stages of kidney disease will typically show no outward signs of illness, although many of these will have detectable abnormalities when laboratory testing is performed. Subtle clinical signs such as weight loss and small changes in thirst may pass unnoticed or their significance be overlooked. For this reason, routine health screening tests are recommended in older cats. The aim of these tests is to identify abnormalities at an early stage such that prompt treatment can be instituted.

The UK based cat charity, the Feline Advisory Bureau has recently classified feline ages into different 'life stages' and correlates this with an approximate human equivalent (page 29).

The American Association of Feline Practitioners (AAFP) and FAB have both developed guidelines regarding the frequency and nature of routine health screening programmes at the different stages of a cat's life. These guidelines advocate more frequent and detailed check-ups as the cat ages. For example, the author follows the FAB Wellcat programme and recommends:

- Blood pressure and urinalysis: annually in cats aged 7 years and over, six monthly in cats aged 15 years and over (consider 6 monthly checks in cats from the age of 11 years):

    - Interpretation of blood pressure results in 'healthy' cats: Since blood pressure can be increased by stress ('white coat hypertension'), interpretation of blood pressure readings is not always straightforward. Where high results are obtained in cats with evidence of ocular damage (e.g.

retinal detachment), anti-hypertensive treatment is recommended. In those cats where there is no evidence of ocular damage in spite of high blood pressure readings, a decision might be made to monitor rather than treat the patient in case stress is the cause of the high readings. Treatment of systemic hypertension is discussed in more detail on pages 39-40

    - Interpretation of urine specific gravity in 'healthy' cats:

        - USG > 1.040: normal result, no further action required

        - USG < 1.035: abnormal result, further investigations recommended (e.g. serum biochemistry, haematology and more detailed urinalysis)

        - USG 1.035-1.040: 'grey' area, repeat measurement and/ or further monitoring recommended

■ Haematology, serum biochemistry, total thyroxine (a test for hyperthyroidism, a common condition affecting elderly cats): annually in cats aged 11 years and over. Blood and urine tests are a good way of identifying common illnesses affecting older cats such as CKD, hyperthyroidism and diabetes mellitus.

How is chronic kidney disease treated?

Treatment varies greatly according to the individual's needs. In the vast majority of cases, treatment proves effective in stabilising a patient and helping to giving them a good quality of life for months or years. Although the damaged kidneys will not recover and CKD will get progressively worse with time, treatment can make an enormous difference to the cat's quality and length of life. For example, if a cat with CKD is fed a renal prescription diet, it will live on average more than twice as long as a cat with CKD which is fed standard catfood.

In general, treatment falls into the following categories:

Treatment of the underlying cause

Where possible, the cause of the kidney disease should be identified and treated. Unfortunately, in the majority of cases, a cause cannot be identified. An example of a treatable cause of kidney disease is a bacterial infection (pyelonephritis). Depending on the severity of the damage caused by the infection, treatment with antibiotics may be able to completely reverse the kidney disease (acute renal failure situations). However, if the disease has been present for some time (weeks or months) there is a high chance of permanent damage which cannot be reversed by the antibiotics. In this situation, the antibiotics are only effective in stopping further worsening of

disease. Even in these cases, treatment is worthwhile and can restore the cat's quality of life and allow the cat to be stabilised for months or years.

Dietary management

Specific dietary therapy (kidney diets) have been shown to dramatically improve the quality of life and survival (length of life) of cats with chronic kidney disease. There are many different types of kidney diets available via veterinarians – examples of widely available brands include:

■ Eukanuba Renal

■ Hill's k/d

■ Purina NF

■ Royal Canin Renal

■ VetXX Specific.

All of the above brands are available in both wet and dry forms, often in more than one flavour.

Home-prepared diets are not recommended as it is very difficult to ensure that these remain balanced and safe for long-term use. Many of the constituents required for preparation of balanced home-prepared diets are not readily available.

A range of commercially available kidney diets (in dry and wet forms) exist to cater for all tastes.

Commercially made kidney diets are modified in several different ways including:

- Restricted levels of phosphate since cats with CKD have a tendency to retain excess amounts of this which can contribute to their feeling unwell. Retention of phosphate in the body (hyperphosphataemia) is common in cats with CKD and is damaging to the kidneys as well as being a major contributor to the development of renal secondary hyperparathyroidism – a condition which is discussed in more detail on pages 16-17

Hand feeding is a useful nursing technique which can be done in both hospitalised and home-cared for patients to help encourage eating. Warming the food slightly, talking to the cat and stroking it can also help.

- Restricted levels of high quality protein which limits the amount of protein breakdown waste products for the ailing kidneys to excrete. Accumulation of protein breakdown products (such as urea and creatinine) is one of the causes of the clinical signs seen in cats with CKD. The main benefit in feeding a low protein diet is therefore management of these clinical signs. One recent study showed that cats with IRIS Stage 2 or 3 renal disease fed a renal prescription diet had a much better quality of life than those fed a standard catfood

- Increased amounts of potassium and B vitamins which CKD cats are vulnerable to losing in their urine. Lack of these nutrients can cause a loss of appetite so it is important to avoid/treat this in cats with CKD. In addition, hypokalaemia (low blood potassium levels) is damaging to kidney function and may worsen the renal disease

- Increased numbers of calories which helps kidney disease cats with a poor appetite to maintain a normal body weight.

The many modifications present in a specially formulated renal prescription diet mean that this acts as a medicine as well as a food.

Kidney diets should be introduced gradually to your cat (e.g. over a period of a few days or weeks) and they should not be offered if your cat is unwell (e.g. vomiting) as your cat might associate the new diet with feeling unwell and refuse to eat the diet again in the future (a phenomenon known as 'food aversion'). Tactics which help to encourage acceptance of the new diet include:

- Offering a small amount of food by hand

- Warming the food gently (so that it is warmer than room temperature but a little cooler than body temperature)

- Adding liquid to the diet to make it softer

- Grooming and sitting with your cat whilst feeding it.

If, in spite of following all of these tactics, your cat refuses to eat the kidney diet then don't despair. View feeding a renal prescription diet as an ideal long-term goal. In the short-term, it is much more important that the cat eats than that it eats the diet of our choice. In the short-term, you may need to offer your cat what they want to eat, rather than what you would prefer! Keep returning to try the renal prescription diets, trying different brands as some cats have very distinct preferences. Some cats will tolerate a diet that is half renal prescription and half standard cat food – this is still better than a diet which is 100% standard catfood.

There are a range of treatments which can be added to standard catfood to make this more closely resemble a renal prescription diet. Whilst not ideal, these methods are better than feeding standard catfood alone. Examples of modifications would include:

- Choosing a senior catfood, where possible, since these diets tend to have lower phosphate and protein levels in them compared to standard adult catfood

- Adding intestinal phosphate binders to the food. These substances combine with phosphate present in the diet and prevent it from being absorbed from the bowel. Phosphate binders are discussed in more detail on pages 37-38

- Adding potassium, B vitamins and fatty acid supplements to the food. A number of different supplements are available from most veterinarians

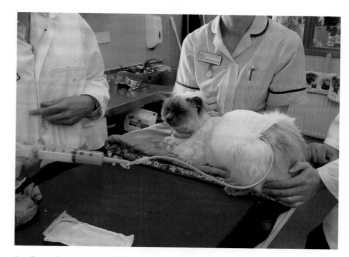

Feeding tubes can be helpful in some patients. This cat has had a gastrostomy tube placed so that liquidised food can be administered directly into the stomach.

- Avoiding acidifying diets – for example some diets designed for dissolving bladder stones would be contra-indicated in a cat with kidney disease since they are more vulnerable to developing metabolic acidosis. If in doubt, ask your veterinarian to check the diet that you are feeding to your cat.

Remember that some food is always better than no food – depending on your cat, you may need to compromise. Again, don't punish yourself if you find yourself in this situation – you can only try your best!

Cats with CKD often have a poor appetite – in some cases this is because of specific complications of their renal disease such as hypokalaemia or nausea related to gastritis. Specific management of these complications, as discussed in the

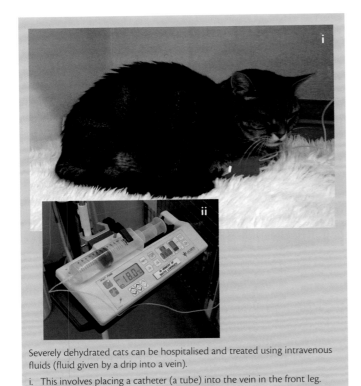

Severely dehydrated cats can be hospitalised and treated using intravenous fluids (fluid given by a drip into a vein).

i. This involves placing a catheter (a tube) into the vein in the front leg. Drip tubing is attached to this.

ii. The fluid can be pumped into the cat using special pumps (such as the syringe pump shown in this picture) or with the aid of gravity.

- Anti-nausea drugs such as maropitant, ondansetron or metaclopramide in case nausea is an issue
- Drugs which reduce the stomach acidity such as famotidine, ranitidine, omeprazole.

In some cases, placing a feeding tube into the oesophagus or stomach is helpful to provide extra food (as shown on page 33). Although anaesthesia and a short period of post-operative hospitalisation are required to place the tube, once in place these can be used for prolonged periods to administer food, liquids and medicines. Feeding tubes are not appropriate for all patients – they should be reserved for those that are otherwise well but where other tactics to increase appetite have failed.

Treatment of dehydration

Dehydrated cats will usually be quiet and withdrawn. A veterinarian may be able to diagnose dehydration on a physical examination of your cat. Signs of dehydration include dry ('tacky') gums and skin tenting – where the skin fails to spring back into place rapidly after being lifted up at the back of the cat's neck. Testing blood levels of salts, proteins and red blood cells can also help to identify dehydration in affected patients since levels of all of these increase in dehydrated cats.

In the early stages following a diagnosis, your veterinarian may suggest that your cat is admitted to the hospital for intravenous fluid therapy – putting your cat on a drip. This can be very effective in improving your cat's condition and giving it a boost before it returns home for more long-term treatment. Intravenous fluid therapy is not something which should be viewed uniformly as a 'bad sign' – many cats will stabilise with this therapy and go on to do very well with standard treatment for their CKD at home.

following pages, usually results in an improvement in the appetite. If your cat's appetite remains poor then your veterinarian may recommend alternative strategies such as

- Appetite stimulants such as cyproheptadine, mirtazapine or anabolic steroids

Encouraging cats to drink and maintain normal hydration is very helpful; moist diets (i.e. canned or pouches) are preferable to dry ones. Some cats prefer eating the dry food and refuse moist diets – this is not necessarily a problem as long as the cat is encouraged to drink plenty. Some of these cats will eat dry food to which water has been added so this is worth a try.

Tips for encouraging your cat to drink more include:

- Ensuring that water supplies are always easily accessible to your cat – for example on every floor of the house and never too far away from where your cat may be sitting or sleeping

- Cats usually prefer to drink from glass, metal or ceramic bowls rather than plastic ones

- Experimenting with different size and shape water bowls – some cats prefer to drink out of tall jugs or glasses rather than bowls. Some cats prefer a different colour bowl to others! Cats do not usually like their whiskers to touch the side of their food or water bowl and they do not like putting their head inside a bowl to drink. The bowl should be wide in diameter

- Cats prefer to drink from bowls which have been filled to the brim - they rarely drink from bowls that are not completely full as this requires them to put their head into the bowl

- Some cats prefer to drink from moving water sources. Examples would include dripping taps, showers and water fountains. A large number of types of water fountains are available through many pet stores and veterinarians

- Offering flavoured water (see below)

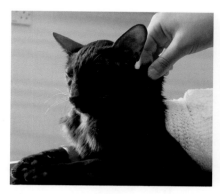

'Skin tenting' is one indication of dehydration. To do this test, a bit of skin – for example the skin of the scruff – is gently lifted up and then let go. In healthy cats, the skin immediately returns to its normal position; in dehydrated cats the skin is slow to return to its normal position or stays standing up ('tented').

- Experimenting with different types of water – e.g. tap water, collected rain water, mineral water to see if your cat prefers water from different sources. Some cats prefer drinking warm water so experimenting with the temperature might also be worthwhile

- Adding water to your cat's food (whether it is wet or dry) – some cats will tolerate a food that resembles soup!

- If your cat has a feeding tube in place then extra fluid can also be given by this route.

Offering flavoured water may encourage your cat to drink more but it must not be a salty liquid as this can increase the risk of systemic hypertension. Examples of ways to do this include:

- Poaching chicken or fish in unsalted water and offering the liquid to your cat as a drink (this can also be frozen and therefore used over a period of time)

- Offering juice from a drained can of tuna/salmon in springwater (not brine) or frozen cooked prawns

It is important to ensure that plenty of water is available to cats with chronic kidney disease as they have increased needs compared to healthy cats. Some cats prefer drinking from interesting receptacles such as this cat who prefers to drink from a jug.

- Liquidising fish or prawns in water to create a fishy broth. Again this can be frozen for future use. Some owners find freezing the liquid in ice cube trays helpful. A cube of frozen broth added to a bowl of water may be enough to stimulate drinking

- Water flavourers are available in some countries and may help cats to drink more.

A guide to encouraging cats to take in more fluids is available in the Free Downloads section of our website www.catprofessional.com.

Some cats may require repeated hospitalisation for intravenous fluid therapy (placing on a drip) to treat dehydration. In these patients, home treatment with subcutaneous fluids (SubQ fluids, administration of fluids under the skin using a needle) can be very helpful to prevent dehydration and hence future hospitalisation. Giving subcutaneous fluids is straightforward in the majority of cases although you will need training from your veterinarian or vet nurse in how to do this. A very useful guide for this technique, written by Dr Andy Sparkes (another UK feline specialist) is available in the Free Downloads section of our website www.catprofessional.com. Cats needing this treatment will typically be prescribed 50-150 ml of fluid per day.

Subcutaneous fluid therapy is beneficial to many cats with CKD. It is especially indicated for those cats that have suffered from repeated bouts of dehydration. In other cats with kidney disease, giving subcutaneous fluids (i.e. fluids extra to their requirements) can be harmful by putting an increased strain on their kidneys and risking overdose with the salts present in the fluids given. Your veterinarian will be able to advise you as to whether your cat is a suitable patient for this therapy. In general, cats needing subcutaneous fluid therapy have one or more of the following in common:

- Their CKD is quite advanced: Stage 3 or 4 on the IRIS scheme: www.iris-kidney.com and producing very dilute urine – urine specific gravity lower than 1.030

- They will only eat dry diets – dehydration is likely since they generally are not good at drinking as much as they need to

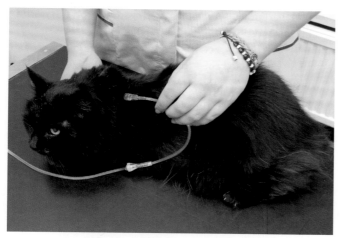

This patient is dehydrated and is receiving subcutaneous fluids (fluid given under the skin). This is a technique which can be done in the hospital. In those patients which are frequently becoming dehydrated, home subcutaneous fluid therapy can be done by the cat's owner following training and advice from a veterinarian.

- They are not good at drinking very much (please note: it is normal for cats to not drink very much but when they have severe kidney disease this changes and they need to drink a lot to stay hydrated)

- They have suffered from dehydration in the past – for example needing hospitalisation and intravenous fluid therapy or constantly suffering from borderline/mild dehydration.

Subcutaneous fluid therapy is a fairly new therapy in some countries so it may not be something that all veterinarians are familiar with. If your veterinarian is not familiar with this therapy then they should find this book and information on our website helpful.

Treatment of specific complications

Some cats may have additional problems that need to be treated. Common problems include:

- Hyperphosphataemia (high blood phosphate levels) – present in around two thirds of patients with CKD: Cats with CKD are vulnerable to hyperphosphataemia since normal regulation of blood phosphate levels requires renal excretion. Hyperphosphataemia is a major contributor to the development of renal secondary hyperparathyroidism and is damaging to the kidneys. Hyperphosphataemia is diagnosed by measuring blood levels of phosphate. Cats with hyperphosphataemia may show clinical signs including loss of appetite, vomiting and depression.

IRIS has defined 'target levels' for blood phosphate levels. Ideally the phosphate should be kept below 1.45 mmol/l (4.5 mg/dl) but as the renal disease worsens, this may not be possible. IRIS therefore have recommended the following target levels for blood phosphate according to the IRIS stage of disease:

- Stage 2: target blood phosphate levels 0.81 - 1.45 mmol/l (2.5 – 4.5 mg/dl)

- Stage 3: target blood phosphate levels 0.81 - 1.61 mmol/l (2.5 – 5 mg/dl)

- Stage 4: target blood phosphate levels 0.81 - 1.94 mmol/l (2.5 – 6 mg/dl).

Cats whose phosphate levels are not completely controlled by dietary therapy and those cats that will not eat the prescription renal diet will need to be prescribed drugs that

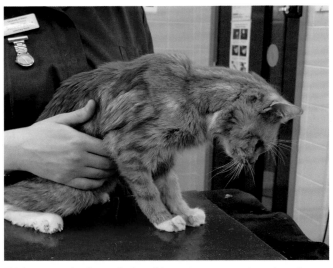

This is an example of ventroflexion of the neck: severe muscle weakness (so much so that this cat cannot lift his head) is present as a result of severe hypokalaemia (abnormally low blood potassium levels).

limit the phosphate absorbed by the bowel. Phosphate binders are typically powders or pastes that need to be added to food before this is offered to the cat (or administered orally very close to a meal time). Phosphate in the diet is bound by the drug, preventing its absorption by the bowel. Examples of phosphate binders available include lantharenol (e.g. Renalzin®), calcium carbonate (e.g. Ipakitine and Epakitin) and aluminium hydroxide (e.g. Alu-cap, Alu-tab).

Phosphate restriction – through the use of renal prescription diets and/or dietary phosphate binders is recommended for all cats in IRIS stages 2, 3 and 4 renal disease. For cats in IRIS stage 2 renal disease, use of a phosphate binder in

combination with a standard cat food may be sufficient to control phosphate levels. For cats in IRIS stages 3 and 4, a renal prescription diet, sometimes with additional phosphate binders, is generally needed to control phosphate levels.

Management of phosphate levels through use of renal prescription diets with additional phosphate binders (if needed) reduces renal secondary hyperparathyroidism and survival times of cats with CKD can be more than doubled. Indeed feeding a low phosphate diet can also reverse consequences of renal secondary hyperparathyroidism such as soft tissue mineralization in some patients. Research studies have shown that cats with kidney disease fed a low phosphate diet are much less vulnerable to progression of their kidney disease – in contrast to CKD cats fed a standard diet, these cats showed no or greatly reduced renal mineralisation or fibrous scarring

- Renal secondary hyperparathyroidism – estimated to be present in at least three quarters of patients with CKD: diagnosis of renal secondary hyperparathyroidism is not straightforward due to the expense of this test and special blood sample requirements as discussed on page 17. The main triggers for development of renal secondary hyperparathyroidism are hyperphosphataemia and reduced production of calcitriol by the kidneys. Any CKD patient with hyperphosphataemia can be assumed to be suffering from renal secondary hyperparathyroidism; some CKD patients with normal blood phosphate levels will also be suffering from renal secondary hyperparathyroidism. For this reason, IRIS has recommended phosphate restriction – as discussed above – for all cats in IRIS stages 2, 3 and 4 renal disease

■ **Hypokalaemia** (low blood potassium levels) – present in around a quarter of patients with CKD: Even with extra potassium provided in the special kidney diet, some cats will need additional potassium supplied as a liquid, powder or tablet. There are a number of potassium supplements which are commercially available for cats – examples of brand names in the UK and US include Tumil K, Kaminox and Amino B + K. Some of these supplements also contain B vitamins and iron. **Hypokalaemia** is diagnosed by measuring blood levels of potassium. Affected cats may have a poor appetite, be more quiet/withdrawn than normal and in severe cases show dramatic muscle weakness. This can be manifested as an inability to lift the head. If very severe, hypokalaemia can worsen kidney function. Fortunately, once corrected (i.e. potassium levels returned to normal) the kidney function improves. Severe hypokalaemia is sometimes best managed by hospitalising your cat and putting it on a high-potassium intravenous drip

Anaemia (a lack of red blood cells) is one of the possible complications of chronic kidney disease and can make the nose (if non-pigmented) appear pale, as in this case.

■ **Systemic hypertension** (high blood pressure) – present in around a fifth of patients with CKD: This is diagnosed by measuring the cat's blood pressure – facilities to do this are now present in most veterinary practices. Examination of the eyes is also important to determine whether or not there is evidence of complications associated with systemic hypertension such as bleeding or retinal detachment. Ocular changes like these are evidence of 'end organ damage' – damage resulting from the high blood pressure. Cats suffering from systemic hypertension can show a range of clinical signs including problems with vision (including blindness), collapse, fits and behavioural changes (e.g. pacing aimlessly,

showing signs of dementia). Sudden blindness is an emergency – prompt treatment can be successful in returning some vision although, sadly, many cats will remain blind for the rest of their life. IRIS currently recommends that anti-hypertensive drugs (medications which lower the blood pressure) are prescribed once systolic blood pressure (the higher of the two blood pressure readings) is persistently above 160 mmHg (mmHg is the abbreviation for millimetres of mercury) in cats with kidney disease. Readings persistently above 180-190 mmHg risk potentially permanent organ damage. The most helpful drugs for treating high blood pressure are amlodipine

Hypersalivation can be associated with nausea, a common complication in cats with CKD

and ACE inhibitors such as benazepril. ACE inhibitors are generally much less effective in reducing blood pressure than amlodipine. An ideal target systolic blood pressure reading for a cat with CKD is below 150 mmHg. The IRIS sub-staging criteria for blood pressure measurements are discussed in more detail on page 28.

As discussed earlier, stress commonly causes a temporary increase in blood pressure ('white coat hypertension'), so it is vital that multiple blood pressure readings are obtained with the cat in as calm and relaxed a state as possible. In those cats where there is no evidence of end organ damage (e.g. ocular abnormalities) in spite of high blood pressure readings, a decision might be made to monitor rather than treat the patient in case stress is the cause of the high readings. In the absence of any known end organ damage IRIS recommendations are that SBP should be treated if:

- Readings are persistently between 160-179 mmHg on several occasions over a two month period

- Readings are persistently 180 mmHg or higher on several occasions over a one to two week period

■ Nausea and vomiting: sickness and vomiting has many causes in the CKD patient – these include:

- Severe azotaemia – best helped by feeding a low protein diet

- Hyperphosphataemia – helped by feeding a low phosphate diet and/or adding phosphate binders (substances which stick to phosphate in the food and stop it from being absorbed by the bowel)

- Acidosis – helped by feeding a prescription kidney diet and/or treating with sodium bicarbonate (not needed in all cats)

- Stomach ulcers – antacids and substances which soothe the lining of the stomach and help healing (known as mucosal protectants) can be very useful. A wide variety of (mostly human) drugs are available for this and include sucralfate – a mucosal protectant, and acid blockers such as ranitidine and famotidine.

Anti-sickness drugs such as mirtazapine and ondansetron can also be helpful in some cats.

■ Anaemia – present in around a third of patients with CKD: Anaemic cats will often be quiet and spend more time sleeping or resting than is normal for them. You may notice that their gums are pale (for example when the cat yawns). Some anaemic cats will show an abnormal appetite – for example eating cat litter, soil or licking concrete. This abnormal appetite is called 'pica'. Anaemia is most accurately diagnosed by a blood test (haematology) which shows low levels of red blood cells.

There are several causes of anaemia in cats with CKD. These include:

- Poor survival of red cells: red blood cells do not live as long as normal in cats with CKD. Unfortunately there is little that can actively be done to treat this. A mild anaemia is therefore quite common in cats with advanced CKD. Cats are very good at adapting to anaemia and adjusting their activity levels accordingly (i.e. spending more time resting)

- Iron deficiency: affected cats may benefit from iron supplementation by solution, tablet or injection. Iron levels can be assessed by a blood test (iron and ferritin tests)

- Erythropoietin deficiency: erythropoietin is a hormone produced by the kidneys which stimulates production of red blood cells by the bone marrow. Levels of production can fall in cats with CKD and supplementation (with a synthetic human erythropoietin) can be helpful in some of these cats. Unfortunately there are some side-effects of this treatment – high blood pressure is one but most importantly the treatment may not work for very long as your cat's body may recognise the erythropoietin as a foreign protein and block it from working. Most clinicians using erythropoietin in their CKD patients recommend that this treatment is not started until the PCV (a measure of anaemia) falls below 20%. It is common to also recommend that iron and Vitamin B12 supplements are given when using this treatment since low levels of either of these substances would be a reason for treatment failure. As always, this is a treatment that should be discussed carefully with your veterinarian

- Stomach ulcers: these can cause blood loss into the bowel leading to anaemia. Drugs which help to soothe the bowel and prevent ulcers from forming can be helpful in some cats – examples include H2-blockers such as ranitidine, famotidine and drugs which help to protect the surface of the bowel such as sucralfate.

Anabolic steroid treatments can also be given to try and stimulate the bone marrow to produce more red blood cells. This is quite a controversial treatment and probably not very effective.

If the anaemia is severe then a short-term treatment option would be a blood transfusion. Unfortunately this treatment only lasts for a few weeks (at the most) but it can be helpful in buying some time whilst other treatments (such as ulcer treatments) are taking effect. Blood transfusion is not an insignificant treatment – and donor cats are not always available – so it requires careful discussion with your veterinarian.

■ Altered blood acidity – acidosis: this is the situation when the blood is more acidic than it should be. Acidosis is quite common in dehydrated CKD patients and is corrected by restoring hydration in most of these. Up to 10% of patients with CKD suffer from metabolic acidosis requiring specific additional treatment. Affected cats are often very ill with no appetite and no energy and may vomit. Prescription kidney diets can be very effective in preventing acidosis from developing. Some cats benefit from additional treatment – for example using sodium bicarbonate to normalise the blood acidity

■ Proteinuria: In mild to moderate cases, this might not be associated with any specific clinical signs. Cats with more severe or long-standing proteinuria may develop abnormally low blood protein levels (hypoproteinaemia) which can cause the face, legs and skin of the chest and/or abdomen to appear puffy or swollen (due to oedema development). Pleural fluid or ascites can also be seen and this can cause, respectively, breathlessness and a swollen/enlarged abdomen. Currently, the best known treatment for proteinuria is an ACE inhibitor such as benazepril – see later section on these drugs

■ Bacterial urinary infection: Around 20-25% of cats with CKD suffer from bacterial urinary tract infections. Unfortunately, many cats with urinary infections do not show specific clinical signs (i.e. the infection is 'silent') and may only show vague clinical signs such as weight loss and lethargy. A small proportion of cats with urinary infections show clinical signs of cystitis including urgency to pass urine, passing small amounts of urine very frequently and passing bloody/smelly urine. Antibiotics are needed to treat urinary tract infections – the type of antibiotic used and the duration of treatment needed will depend on the bacteria causing the infection. Determining which antibiotic treatments are suitable requires culture of the urine to grow the bacteria and see what antibiotic it is sensitive to (a culture and sensitivity test).

Cats receiving multiple therapies can be difficult to medicate. Medicating with multiple drugs can be made easier by using empty gelatine capsules available from a veterinarian or pharmacist. The capsule is opened, the appropriate drugs are added and then the capsule is closed again. This means that it is possible to dose a cat with two or more medicines in one go – likely to be much more popular with the cat than giving multiple pills. Giving multiple medications can increase the risk of side-effects through drug interactions which is something for you and your veterinarian to discuss and be aware of when working out a treatment regime for your cat. For example, some medications can prevent absorption of others so always discuss timing of treatment administration with your veterinarian. If you are finding it difficult to medicate your cat ask your veterinarian to prioritise which treatments are most important so that you can ensure that your cat is getting the most important ones everyday.

After any tablet or capsule medication is given the cat should be offered food or given a small amount of water to encourage the tablet to travel to the stomach. This is to prevent tablets or capsules from sitting in the food pipe (oesophagus) for prolonged periods where they can cause irritation and potentially serious and long-lasting problems such as strictures (narrowing of the food pipe).

What about ACE (angiotensin converting enzyme) inhibitors such as benazepril and chronic kidney disease?

In addition to the special diet and the other measures outlined above, ACE inhibitors such as benazepril have been advocated for the treatment of cats with chronic kidney disease. Data from clinical trials suggests that CKD cats receiving this therapy have a better quality of life, a better appetite, a reduction in the amount of protein they lose in their urine and may live a little longer. ACE inhibitors also lower the blood pressure and so may be prescribed as an anti-hypertensive therapy (a treatment for cats with high blood pressure). The cats that benefit most from use of an ACE inhibitor are:

- Cats losing protein into their urine (proteinuric cats). CKD cats with a UPC result persistently above 0.4 are candidates for this treatment as long as other causes of proteinuria such as urinary tract infections and other non renal illnesses have been ruled out. The greatest proven benefits of ACE inhibitors in treating proteinuria are reported for cats with UPC ratios above 1.0

- Cats with high blood pressure. When used alone, ACE inhibitors are not potent treatments for systemic hypertension – often these drugs need to be given in

(i) Syringing a small amount of water after giving a pill or capsule helps the medication to travel to the stomach quickly and without causing any irritation to the oesophagus (food pipe). Alternatively (ii) a small amount of butter can be put on the cat's nose – licking this off also helps any pills and capsules to travel quickly to the stomach.

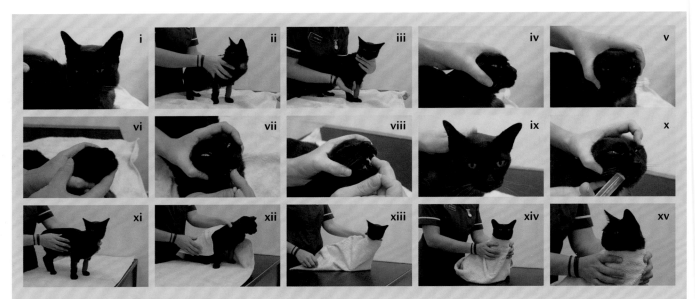

Medicating cats with pills or tablets

(i) try and ensure that your cat remains calm and relaxed; (ii) and (iii) the person restraining the cat gently holds the front legs so that they cannot come up and prevent pills being given or scratch you; (iv) and (v) make your forefingers and thumb into an arch shape and place this over the angle of the jaw holding the bony angle of the jaw firmly (this should not hurt your cat at all); (vi) tip your cat's head back gently so that the nose points to the ceiling; (vii) holding the pill between your thumb and forefinger gently open the jaw using your third finger; (viii) place the pill as far to the back of the mouth as possible; (ix) release your cat's head and allow them to swallow naturally, (x) syringe a small amount of water after giving the pill or allow your cat to have something to eat. (xi)–(xv) If your cat is very wriggly then placing them between your legs whilst you kneel on the floor or wrapping in a towel can help.

combination with a calcium channel blocker (such as amlodipine)

- Cats in stable CKD (ACE inhibitors should not be used in newly diagnosed cases or in cats that are dehydrated).

Your veterinarian should be able to advise you as to whether an ACE inhibitor is indicated in your cat.

What about calcitriol and chronic kidney disease?

Calcitriol is a controversial treatment for cats with chronic kidney disease – depending on where you live your veterinarian may or may not advocate this treatment. For example, it is rarely used in the UK although quite common in certain practices in the USA.

Calcitriol is a naturally produced hormone that helps to control calcium levels in the body. It has been proposed as a treatment for cats with CKD as a method of normalising levels of parathyroid hormone which tend to be high in cats with this condition. Renal secondary hyperparathyroidism (excessively high levels of parathyroid hormone) is common in cats with CKD and is thought to be harmful by exacerbating progression of their renal disease and making them feel ill (e.g. causing nausea and a poor appetite). Feeding a prescription kidney diet low in phosphate helps, as can phosphate binders, but calcitriol is also suggested by some clinicians to be useful in treating the hyperparathyroidism. Some veterinarians feel that cats treated with calcitriol are brighter, have a better appetite, are more active and live longer. However, opinion is divided, there are some concerns over side-effects (mainly the risk of causing hypercalcaemia – an increase in blood calcium levels which can be very harmful) and there is no published scientific evidence to back-up the claims made advocating the use of calcitriol in cats.

Minstrel, a cat with diabetes melllitus and CKD.

Can CKD cats with other illnesses still receive treatment?

It is common for cats with CKD to suffer from other illnesses – in particular those that are common in older cats such as hyperthyroidisim (overactive thyroid gland), diabetes mellitus ('sugar diabetes') and dental problems. Assessment and management of these illnesses can be complicated by the presence of CKD. In some situations, sub-optimal treatment of one condition might be needed to prevent another condition from decompensating.

Hyperthyroidism and CKD: Assessment and treatment of hyperthyroid cats with CKD is often complicated. All treatments for hyperthyroidism have the potential to worsen kidney function. This is because all treatments of hyperthyroidism cause a reduction in blood flow to the kidneys. This has the

Intravenous fluid therapy provides helpful support for a cat with CKD undergoing anaesthesia or surgery.

potential to 'unmask' or reveal kidney disease that was not previously known about and to worsen pre-existing kidney disease. Unfortunately there is no way to predict which cats will suffer renal problems following treatment of their thyroid disease. For this reason, medical treatment of hyperthyroidism is recommended initially since this is a reversible treatment which can be reduced or stopped if problems are seen. Hyperthyroidism is discussed in much more detail in another Cat Professional publication 'Caring for a cat with hyperthyroidism'.

Diabetes mellitus and CKD: one of the difficulties posed in a cat suffering from both of these conditions is the current recommendation for very different diets. Whilst a low phosphate and low protein diet is recommended for cats with CKD, a high protein and low carbohydrate diet is generally recommended for cats with diabetes. In this situation, the best approach is usually to concentrate on whichever condition is the biggest

concern for the cat – for example if the renal disease is very mild, a phosphate binder added to a diabetic diet might be most appropriate. As always, your veterinarian is in the best position to advise you regarding the treatment of your cat.

Anaesthesia of a cat with CKD needs to be handled very carefully as any lowering in the blood pressure, which is common under anaesthesia, can reduce the blood flow to the kidneys and result in problems. This is a particular concern in cats with CKD requiring dental surgery. Anaesthetic risks can be reduced by measures including:

■ Planning the procedure, where possible, performing renal assessment (including detailed blood tests) so that any abnormalities which might affect the procedure (e.g. anaemia, electrolyte abnormalities) can be identified and corrected, where possible

■ Use of anaesthetic regimes which help to support the blood pressure (ie help to keep the blood pressure in the normal range)

■ Ensuring that the patient is not dehydrated at the time of anaesthesia, for example, by admitting the cat and placing it on intravenous fluids (a drip) before the anaesthetic is given. For some patients, it is beneficial to admit them and place them on a drip 24-48 hours before the anaesthetic is given

■ Continuing intravenous fluids throughout the anaesthetic and recovery periods

■ Monitoring blood pressure throughout the anaesthesia and administering other treatments, if needed, to support the blood pressure

Weight loss is a very common consequence of **chronic kidney disease**

- Pre-operative antibiotics are usually recommended in CKD cats undergoing dental surgery

- Food and water should be offered to the cat as soon as it has recovered from anaesthesia.

How can I give my cat the best quality and length of life possible?

For many cats, once stabilised, their care is not difficult, time-consuming or stressful and it is possible to provide a good quality of life for months or years.

Regular monitoring and vigilance for development of new problems are essential in ensuring the best care of your cat. Of all of the treatments discussed, kidney diets have been proven to be the most effective so all efforts should be concentrated on persuading your cat to eat these – even if it takes months to achieve this aim! However, it is always more important that your cat eats than that it eats a kidney diet so if they are not interested in the special diet, they should be offered a cat food which they will eat. Senior diets are preferable to routine cat food as these have lower levels of protein and phosphate in them – more information on this can also be found in the section on Dietary Management, pages 31-34.

In stable patients, check-ups should be arranged initially on a monthly basis at which time the following should be done at least every 3 months:

- History taking and physical examination:

  - Aim of these tests: to assess the progress of the patient since the last check-up and to look for evidence of problems associated with the CKD e.g. pale gums (which could indicate anaemia), mouth ulcers, bleeding into the eyes or retinal detachment (which could indicate high blood pressure), dehydration, weight loss etc. In a stable CKD patient, these check-ups will not always involve blood or urine samples and should not be stressful (or expensive) for you or your cat

A check-up every 3 months ensures that any problem is detected promptly and can therefore be addressed quickly.

- Frequency of check-up required: initially monthly but in the longer term, depending on the progress of an individual patient, it may be possible to stretch out the period between check-ups. I advocate that these check-ups should be done a minimum of every 3 months in cats with CKD

- Why are such regular check-ups needed in all cats?

  - A veterinary examination is the best way of detecting changes which might not be obvious at home since the care provider is seeing their cat every day. For example, weight loss commonly goes unnoticed by carers (unless it becomes quite dramatic) as it is impossible to observe a small daily amount of weight loss when you are seeing your cat every day. I have seen many cats that have lost 10-20% of their body weight since the last check-up but whose owners are unaware of any change in their

condition (or even think that their cat has gained weight!). Imagine how much weight loss this would be for you and hence how serious a consequence this could be for your cat!

  - A check-up every 3 months ensures that any problem, such as weight loss, is detected promptly and can therefore be treated quickly

  - 3 monthly check–ups maintain good contact with your veterinarian. Good teamwork between you and your veterinarian will lead to the best care and hence, best outcome for your cat

■ Blood pressure measurement (where possible) and eye examination (to look for evidence of high blood pressure) should be done following a diagnosis of CKD. Examination of the eyes is something that can easily be done at the general check-ups and therefore can continue to be done every 3 months or whenever the cat comes in for a check-up.

- Aim of these tests: to identify and treat high blood pressure promptly. If left untreated, high blood pressure risks serious consequences such as permanent blindness, worsening kidney disease and death

- Frequency of check-up required:

  - If blood pressure is normal at the initial check then I would advocate a second check within the first two months to ensure that high blood pressure is not being overlooked. If still normal at this point then I would reduce the frequency of blood pressure reassessments to a minimum of two check-ups a year

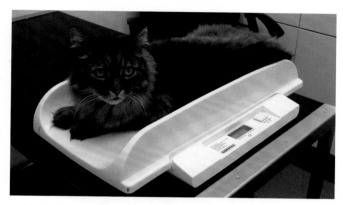

Weight checks are vital to assess progress of cats with **chronic kidney disease**. Small sets of scales, which can be housed in the vets' consulting room, are ideal for this purpose.

- In those cats needing treatment for **systemic hypertension**, blood pressure needs to be checked more frequently – especially during the initial period of treatment. Once blood pressure is stable subsequent check-ups can be done less frequently. This is something that I do gradually according to the patient – for example reducing the frequency of blood pressure check-ups to every three or four months if very stable

- Why are such regular check-ups needed in all cats? **Systemic hypertension** is often referred to as the 'silent killer' – blood pressure checks ensure that high blood pressure is identified quickly helping to prevent development of consequences associated with this condition

- Repeat laboratory tests:
  - Aim of these tests:
    - To check whether treatment for complications of the kidney disease (e.g. **hyperphosphataemia**) has been successful or whether it needs adjusting
    - To check whether new complications of the **CKD** have appeared
    - To monitor progression of the kidney disease itself
  - Frequency of check-up required:
    - As indicated by the results of a history and **physical examination** – for example if your veterinarian is suspicious of **anaemia** (for example if your cat's gums appear very pale) then a **haematology** profile may be indicated to assess the numbers of red blood cells and haemoglobin content
    - Once a patient is stable, repeat blood and urine tests are generally indicated every 6 months. In very stable patients this interval can be increased to 12 months.

Remember – not all medications mentioned in this book are veterinary approved ('licensed') for the treatment of cats and there are differences between countries as to what is available. Your vet should discuss this with you, where applicable to your cat.

Cats should be returned for check-ups sooner if you have any concerns. Specific causes for concern include:

- Sudden deterioration or loss of vision
- Loss of appetite which persists for more than 24 hours
- Severe weakness – e.g. unable to raise the head ('ventroflexion of the neck') which may indicate hypokalaemia
- Vomiting more frequently
- Severe lethargy/listlessness.

Are routine vaccinations and worming still needed in cats with chronic kidney disease?

Cats with stable and well managed chronic kidney disease still benefit from routine preventative health care such as vaccination. All illnesses – including CKD – reduce a cat's ability to fight infections so they will be more vulnerable to severe illness if they contract an infection. Visits to a veterinary practice can be stressful (which can lower immunity) and risk contact with infectious agents.

As always, follow your veterinarian's advice on what is most appropriate for your cat. For example, an indoor-only cat that has no access to hunting or fleas does not generally need to be de-wormed and de-fleaed.

What is the prognosis (long-term outlook) for cats with chronic kidney disease?

The long-term outlook for cats with chronic kidney disease is very variable, ranging from a few weeks to many years following diagnosis. CKD is always considered to be a progressive disease – i.e. it will get worse with time although the rate of progression varies between individual cats.

Prognosis is dependent upon the cause of the disease, the rate of worsening of disease, concurrent medical problems and the severity of the consequences of the kidney disease. Owner and veterinary monitoring of the affected cat helps to assess the severity of the disease and its rate of progression which ensures that the cat receives all of the treatments it needs to help maintain good health. Care of affected cats at home can be very rewarding and is helpful in ensuring that the cat has the best quality of life for as long as possible.

Morgan, a cat with chronic kidney disease and a happy outcome!

Morgan, a part-Persian cat, was presented to me as a referral patient in December 2004 when she had just turned four years old. Her owner, Jacquie continues her story…

So much has happened since Morgan was first diagnosed with chronic kidney disease and we were told she had a week or two – at most – to live. That was back in October 2004, and I'm happy to report that she is still with us today, more than 6 years later – happy, playful and queen of all she surveys. As I write this in February 2011, she has a shiny black coat, bright amber eyes and weighs in at just over 4kg. To look at her, you'd never know there was anything wrong with her. She looks like a normal, healthy cat. I hope and pray this continues for a very long time, but I take nothing for granted. Each new day with her is a blessing.

Morgan and her sister Merlin didn't have the best of starts in life. They came to me at just 8 weeks old, tiny little scraps of terrified black fluff, totally unsocialised and afraid of everything. Over the following days, the kittens slowly learnt to trust me, and Morgan in particular bonded with me and became my little black shadow. For the first few years, everything seemed normal, just the usual vet visits for neutering, health checks and vaccinations. Then in mid-2004 things began to change. Hindsight is always perfect, but back then, I didn't understand the warning signs. Morgan's coat changed gradually over time, and her sleek black fur became rough, dry, and almost rust-coloured. She also started to lose weight, but again, this was very gradual and I didn't think too much about it at the time. Morgan had always been a nervous, finicky cat, quick to go off her food.

Then in October 2004, she began vomiting, stopped eating entirely and became very sick and depressed. Anything I did manage to get her to eat, she threw back up again. She spent all her time asleep or hovering over her water bowl. I took her to the vets and the vet examined her. He noted that she was thin and dehydrated, and kept her in for blood testing and fluids. Several hours later, I got that devastating call. Morgan had chronic kidney disease, it was incurable, and it was terminal. She maybe had a week or so – at most – to live.

She was still only *three years old*!

I was grief-stricken, devastated and guilty. Why hadn't I noticed the symptoms earlier? Was it something I'd done? Could I have prevented it? Morgan was so young! How could she have chronic kidney disease? Wasn't that a problem only older cats faced? Was there no way to manage it? The vet was sympathetic, but very downbeat about her chances. Morgan's blood test results showed that the measurements for kidney disease, notably her creatinine and urea levels, were dangerously high. Her creatinine was around 1400 µmol/l (16 mg/dl) and her urea around 79 mmol/l (220 mg/dl).

Morgan was hospitalised and put on a drip, and four days later, her test results were much improved. She was given a B-vitamin injection, a steroid injection and sent home with dry prescription food. Against all expectations, Morgan seemed okay for the next 5 weeks. She refused to eat the renal food of course, and was picky about food in general, but she seemed in remarkably good spirits. Then, the day after a check-up which showed her

Morgan at the time of first presentation

creatinine and urea both only mildly elevated, she crashed again, almost as bad as before, and once again, her numbers went sky high almost overnight.

The vet put her back on a drip, but he didn't have any answers for us or any suggestions. I felt completely helpless and alone. Although he hadn't said it yet, I knew what he was thinking. In his view, there was no hope.

At this point, I began my own research. I came across several websites that all described the same treatments used to help stabilise the CKD cat and make it feel better, treatments that

were very common in the US, but not so common in the UK. The site that helped me the most was www.felinecrf.org , a site written by a knowledgeable layperson who has lived in the UK and the US, and has experience of how vets treat CKD cats in both countries. I also joined several online mailing lists for people with cats who had CKD, and I asked other UK people if they knew of any good vets with experience of treating CKD in cats. One mentioned Sarah Caney, who had just moved to within driving distance of where I lived. I looked her up, asked my vet for a referral and took Morgan down to see her in mid-December 2004.

Sarah Caney saved Morgan's life. I have no doubt about that. The delays in getting the proper treatments meant that Morgan's problems had gone from very bad to even worse. Her creatinine peaked at over 1800 (20 mg/dl), she had severe metabolic acidosis and her weight had dropped to a terrifying 2.65kg. It was amazing she was still alive. She was hospitalised again for a week, and in the days and weeks that followed, we had some further ups and downs until we finally got her acidosis under control, but since January 2005, Morgan has been treated entirely at home, with occasional vet check-ups and minor adjustments in her medication. She gets subcutaneous fluids once a day and an empty gel capsule at the same time which we fill with the following medications: sodium bicarbonate (for the acidosis), aluminium hydroxide (phosphate binder), ranitidine (for excess stomach acid), ondansetron (an anti-sickness drug that has worked very well for Morgan), cyproheptadine (an appetite enhancer), and B-vitamins and iron (for mild anaemia). More recently, we added omeprazole to the mix on a temporary basis, when the ranitidine alone wasn't effective enough.

Giving Morgan her medications was very daunting at first. However, it wasn't as difficult as it first seemed. The key thing, once your vet has shown you how to administer fluids and medications properly, is to figure out what routine works best for you and your cat. Morgan has always been very easy to carry and has always loved sitting in boxes, so placing her in a cardboard box lined with a fluffy towel, sitting on a chair in the bathroom proved the ideal place for her medications, a routine we still use over 6 years later.

All of Morgan's medications take just 5 minutes, once a day. We keep to the same routine every day, including the words and tone we use as we go to collect her for her medications. We don't try to hide anything from her. She knows exactly what is happening and when, and this keeps her stress levels to a minimum. I can't say she likes it much, and I don't blame her for that, but she never struggles, never fights or hides. I can give Morgan all her medications myself with no help at all, and aside from those 5 minutes a day, Morgan lives a normal cat's life.

I've also been able to train family and friends to look after her in just the same way, which means I'm able to go away on holiday.

I know we've been lucky. After our referral to Sarah, Morgan has received the very best of vet care, first from Sarah and then from another specialist vet, when Sarah moved away from our area.

My best advice to owners if they are concerned about the treatments their cat is receiving is to ask for a referral to a vet with specialist knowledge of CKD and any other medical issues your cat may be suffering from. General practitioner (GP) vets can be good, but they may not know all possible treatments for every disease. If there is no CKD specialist in your area, then try to find a GP vet who is open minded, willing to go the extra mile to learn more about CKD treatments and who is prepared to work with you (for more than the usual five minutes of GP consultation time!) to find the right combination of treatments to give your cat the best possible quality of life, despite the diagnosis of kidney disease. Some specialists, including Sarah, offer telephone consultations which can be very helpful in reviewing treatment programmes.

For us, stabilising Morgan, finding the right vet and the right combination of treatments was by far the hardest part. Learning how to pill and how to give subcutaneous fluids was easy in comparison.

Any owner or vet reading this booklet is clearly trying to give the CKD cat under their care the best chance possible, so all I'll say in conclusion is:

(1) Don't assume that something (like giving pills or using needles) is too difficult or stressful for cat or owner – you won't know until you try;

(2) Think outside the box in giving medications, as no cat is the same; for instance, if your cat hates liquid medication, work with your vet to find alternatives - in our case, it was pill versions we could pop in an empty gel cap; and

(3) Try to persuade your cat to eat a wet renal diet, but if they won't touch it, don't panic. Morgan eats normal commercial

dry cat food and refuses to touch any renal food, wet or dry, even with appetite enhancers. I give phosphate binders as part of Morgan's regime, and try to find commercial cat foods she likes with the lowest possible phosphate levels.

Ultimately, we're doing this to give our cats quality of life in the time they have left, and what I'm trying to show with this case study is how this can be achieved with the benefit of home treatments, in our case for many, many years. One day, there will come a point when Morgan's quality of life is compromised with no hope of improvement. Then a decision will have to be made, but thankfully, we haven't reached that stage yet.

Given Morgan's very severe kidney issues, no-one really expected her to live as long as she has, even with home treatments, but boy, has she proved everyone wrong!

Back home when stable.

Morgan looking well at home in 2010.

Author's note: very sadly Morgan lost her battle with kidney disease on 24 January 2012, more than seven years after she was first diagnosed with CKD. This book is dedicated in her honour.

A good relationship with your veterinarian is vital to the care and wellbeing of your cat with CKD. It is important therefore that you feel able to discuss all of your concerns openly. Your veterinarian is in the best position to advise you regarding specific questions on treatment and prognosis – for example whether or not your cat could benefit from treatment with subcutaneous fluids or whether certain drugs are indicated. You should feel able to ask your veterinarian any questions and they should be able to explain things to you clearly in a way you can understand.

If you feel that the relationship you have with your veterinarian is not answering your concerns then you can ask to see another veterinarian within the practice, or look for another practice. Do not feel uncomfortable if you want to do this – your veterinarian should not mind and it is within your rights to choose the veterinarian you feel is best able to look after your cat. It is always worthwhile asking if there is anyone in the practice who is particularly interested in cat medicine. The UK cat charity, the Feline Advisory Bureau, has a list of vet practices (mainly in the UK) that are members of the charity (see http://www.fabcats. org/owners/choosing_a_vet/practice_members1.php) which is a good indication of enthusiasm and knowledge in feline medicine. The American Association of Feline Practitioners also has an online directory of member practices at http://www.catvets.com/findadoctor/findadoctor.aspx. A number of feline-only practices exist in many countries and you may be fortunate in finding one of these in your area.

Veterinarians specialising in feline medicine can be contacted by your veterinarian for further advice, if needed, or referral to a specialist can be arranged.

In order for your veterinarian to be able to provide the level of care you are looking for with your cat, they will need to understand things from your perspective. For example:

- Will you be able to medicate your cat at home or is this out of the question (for example because your cat is very feisty or because you have severe arthritis in your fingers)? Will giving some medications be possible (e.g. dietary treatment) but others not possible (e.g. tablets)?

- What are your expectations for your cat? For example, would you prefer minimum intervention accepting a potentially shorter time with your cat or are you keen for your cat to have every possible medical treatment?

- Are finances limited in which case certain treatments may be too expensive? Your veterinarian will be able to advise you on the likely cost of treating your cat

- Are there any particular treatments which you object to being used in your cat?

Once both of you know what your expectations are then it should be possible to jointly work out a treatment plan that is appropriate for you and your cat. It is important to remember that all treatment plans can be modified – at any time – and that anything you agree to can be changed, if needed, in the future.

Knowing when to say 'goodbye'

How long has my cat got before he/she dies or needs putting to sleep (euthanasia)?

This is an impossible question for me to answer as it varies enormously from cat to cat. Lots of cats can live a normal quality of life for some years after a diagnosis of CKD has been made. Sadly some die or need to be put to sleep (euthanased) soon after the diagnosis is made. Your veterinarian is in the best position to advise on your own cat and its likely prognosis.

Will I know when it's time to say goodbye to my cat and let him/her go?

It is very rare for an elderly sick cat to die painlessly in their sleep – much though most owners would wish this to happen. Dying tends to be a slow and distressing process and it is far kinder to intervene and ask a veterinarian to put your cat to sleep (euthanase it) when the time has come than let your cat suffer a prolonged and possibly painful death. It is therefore a sad inevitability that one day you are likely to have to decide that your cat needs putting to sleep. For many owners the thought of making this decision is painful and worrying. Most owners feel that their cat should be put to sleep once their quality of life has deteriorated and there is no veterinary treatment that can help to improve this. Your veterinarian should be able to support and guide you in making this decision – if you are at all worried then consult them for advice.

Quality of life is not easy to judge but guidelines include:

- Behaviour:

  a) Is your cat still behaving in its normal way – following its usual routines and activities (e.g. spending the same amount of time grooming)? Is your cat interacting with you as normal?

  b) OR, has your cat become withdrawn and quiet, hiding, not interested in going outside (if normally allowed out) or in interacting with you and other animals in the home?

- Appetite:

  a) Is your cat still interested in food?

  b) OR, has their appetite disappeared and getting them to eat has become a struggle?

- Toileting behaviour:

  a) Is your cat still passing urine and faeces in the litter tray (or outside in the garden) as is normal for them?

  b OR, has your cat started to pass urine and faeces in other places (such as on their bed or on your carpets and flooring)?

- Vocalisation:

  a) Is your cat as chatty as normal?

  b) OR, has there been a change in the amount of vocalisation (increase or decrease) or the sound that your cat makes when miaowing?

- Pain or distress:

  a) Does your cat seem happy and comfortable?

  b) OR, have you seen any sign of pain or discomfort – for example signs of fear or aggression when being handled or sitting in the same place for hours with a glazed expression?

- Signs of illness:

  a) Is your cat free of signs of illness?

  b) OR, is it suffering from signs of illness such as vomiting, weight loss or constipation?

If you answer b) to any of the above questions then you should consult your veterinarian for advice on whether there are any treatments that can help your cat to regain its quality of life. If there are, you need to consider whether to give these treatments a try before making any final decisions.

What does euthanasia involve?

For most veterinarians, euthanasia involves giving an overdose injection of a barbiturate anaesthetic agent intravenously, usually into a vein in the front leg. Once the injection is started, the cat will lose consciousness within a few seconds and the heart should stop within a few minutes. Occasionally, the veins of the front leg can be very fragile and difficult to access so alternative injection sites need to be used – these include the kidneys and the liver. In any case, the process should be quick and painless.

Although the majority of cats are put to sleep at a veterinary practice, most veterinarians will be happy to come to an owner's home to do this, if desired.

What happens to my cat's body after they die or are euthanased (put to sleep)?

In general the options will be:

- Burying your cat's body at home

- Asking your veterinarian to arrange cremation of your cat's body. If desired, you can ask for an individual cremation to be performed and for the ashes to be returned to you.

Your veterinarian will be able to discuss these options with you. It is worthwhile considering how you would like your cat to be put to sleep (should the need arise) and what you would like to happen to their body while your cat is still well. This will save you the added distress of these decisions when your cat dies.

How to cope with losing your cat

Is there support available for me in my grief?

Losing a beloved cat is always going to be a traumatic and distressing experience and you are likely to go through several acknowledged stages of grief. These include denial, anger, guilt, hopelessness/depression and finally acceptance. Most people experience at least two of these stages. Care providers of cats with terminal illnesses such as CKD may start to go through this process as soon as the diagnosis is made. Where this is the case, a further stage of grief – 'bargaining' – may also be experienced where an owner is keen for their cat to live to a certain point (for example, please let them live through Christmas so we can have this time together).

Hopefully you will have friends and family that will be able to provide some support to you throughout this period. If you don't, then consider talking to the veterinarians or nurses at your veterinary practice, your doctor or a priest – all of whom should be able to offer support. There may be local support groups available (your veterinary practice should know about these) and there is also a UK helpline available for dedicated pet bereavement counselling, the Pet Bereavement Support Service (PBSS): 0800 096 6606 open from 8.30am to 8.30pm daily. All calls are free and confidential. The PBSS also offers an e-mail support service: pbssmail@bluecross.org.uk

More information on this service is available on: http://www. bluecross.org.uk/2083/Pet-Bereavement-Support-Service.html

What about my other cat/s – are they likely to grieve?
Yes, it is possible. As with people, cats can show grief at the loss of a companion. The behaviour of a cat following the loss of a house-mate is very variable and unpredictable. Some cats seem completely unaffected by the loss, some appear happier once they are on their own whilst others may show signs of grief such as sleeping less, not eating, urinating in inappropriate places, appearing to look for their lost companion and vocalising more or losing all interest in life.

This process can affect cats (and other animals) for up to a year following their loss. In most cases, signs of grief will disappear within 6 months. You can help affected cats in the following ways:

- Keep routines in the home the same

- If your cat has lost its appetite then try hand-feeding food that has been slightly warmed (to just below body temperature). Consult your veterinarian if your cat has not eaten for three or more days. A complete loss of appetite can cause a potentially fatal liver disease called hepatic lipidosis

- Provide reassurance to your cat by spending more time with them, grooming them, talking to them and playing with them

- Don't immediately get a new cat. Although some cats will crave the company of a new companion, many cats will be more upset and distressed if a new cat is introduced too soon. Many cats prefer to be in single cat households and it is impossible to predict what they will feel about a newcomer. So, if your cat seems happy after the loss of a house-mate I would not get another cat. If, on the other hand, you are keen to expand the home or feel that your cat is 'lonely' then I would advise waiting for at least a couple of months before considering introducing a new cat.

More information on feline bereavement is available on the FAB website: http://www.fabcats.org/owners/euthanasia/bereavement.html. The FAB also has advice on introducing a new cat which could be helpful once a decision has been made to get another cat: http://www.fabcats.org/behaviour/introducing/index.php

Useful websites

Several websites have been mentioned in this publication and you might find these interesting to look at:

General cat advice

The Feline Advisory Bureau http://www.fabcats.org

The Blue Cross http://www.bluecross.org.uk/

Cats Protection http://www.cats.org.uk/

The Royal Society for the Prevention of Cruelty to Animals http://www.rspca.org.uk/

American Association of Feline Practitioners http://www.catvets.com/

Choosing a veterinary practice

http://www.fabcats.org/owners/choosing_a_vet/practice_members1.php

http://www.catvets.com/findadoctor/findadoctor.aspx

Information on kidney disease

http://www.iris-kidney.com

http://www.felinecrf.com/index.htm

http://www.felinecrf.org/

Separate articles on giving subcutaneous fluids to your cat and encouraging it to take in more fluids

http://www.catprofessional.com/free_downloads.html

Bereavement support

http://www.bluecross.org.uk/2083/Pet-Bereavement-Support-Service.html

http://www.fabcats.org/owners/euthanasia/bereavement.html

http://www.fabcats.org/owners/euthanasia/

Introducing a new cat to the home

http://www.fabcats.org/behaviour/introducing/index.php

Glossary of terms used by vets

Term	Definition
Acidosis (metabolic acidosis)	The blood is more acidic than normal. This is one potential consequence of chronic kidney disease and can make affected cats lose their appetite, feel nauseous and generally off colour.
Acute renal failure – ARF	Also referred to as acute kidney disease. Sudden loss of kidney function which can be caused by one or more of the following: ■ Reduced blood supply to the kidneys (so called pre-renal ARF). Causes include heart failure and dehydration ■ Damage to the kidneys themselves (renal or intrinsic ARF). Causes include poisoning e.g. antifreeze (ethylene glycol), eating lilies, grapes or raisins ■ Failure of urine excretion due to a blockage in the urethra (tube from the bladder to the outside) or rupture of the bladder. This is called post-renal ARF. Although many causes of ARF are fully treatable (and the kidney damage can be reversed), if severe and untreated, ARF can progress to CKD.
Anaemia	A reduction in the numbers of red blood cells in the circulation. Red blood cells (also known as erythrocytes) carry oxygen to the tissues of the body so anaemic cats will often be weak and listless. Anaemias are subdivided into: ■ Regenerative anaemias: ones in which the bone marrow (which manufactures red blood cells) is responding to the anaemia and trying to correct this ■ Non-regenerative anaemias: ones in which the bone marrow response (ability to produce more new erythrocytes) is insufficient or absent.
Anaesthesia	Providing a state of unconsciousness, muscle relaxation and loss of pain sensation using certain drugs (usually a combination of intravenous administration and by gas inhalation).
Anorexia	Complete loss of appetite in contrast to inappetence which is a decrease in the appetite.
Ascites	Accumulation of fluid in the abdominal cavity (the space around all of the abdominal organs).
Azotaemia	accumulation of protein breakdown products such as urea and creatinine in the blood. Measurement of urea and creatinine levels is used to diagnose kidney disease.

Term	Definition
Biochemistry	Refers to blood tests of organ function (e.g. urea and creatinine), blood salt levels and protein levels.
Biopsy	Collection and laboratory analysis of a sample of tissue e.g. kidney biopsy.
Calcitriol	Calcitriol is a naturally produced hormone that helps to control calcium levels in the body.
Chronic interstitial nephritis	See nephritis.
Chronic kidney disease (CKD)	Inadequate kidney function which has been present for at least 2 weeks. This is considered to be a progressive condition – it will get worse with time – although the speed of progression is variable.
Clinical examination	Examination of body systems by a veterinarian or nurse. Typically this includes listening to the chest, opening the mouth and feeling the abdomen.
Clinical signs	The term used to describe what we would call our 'symptoms' if we were the cat e.g. sickness, loss of appetite.
Creatinine	One of the protein breakdown products that is normally excreted by the kidneys and hence accumulates in the blood of cats with kidney disease. Blood creatinine is derived from muscle turnover and levels are lower in cats in poor muscle condition. Blood levels of creatinine may increase following a meal and are high in cats suffering from dehydration.
Cystitis	Inflammation of the urinary bladder (where urine is stored before urination). One cause would be a bacterial infection of the urine.
Cystocentesis	Technique of urine collection using a needle and syringe. The needle is passed through the skin and into the bladder from which urine is collected.
Electrolyte	Blood salt – the most important blood salts in cats with chronic kidney disease are sodium, potassium, calcium and phosphate.
Erythropoietin	A hormone produced by the kidneys which stimulates production of red blood cells by the bone marrow. A lack of erythropoietin is one cause of the anaemia (low red blood cell numbers) which can be seen in cats with chronic kidney disease.

Term	Definition
Euthanasia	Also referred to as 'putting to sleep' this is the term used when a veterinarian ends a cat's life. This non-painful treatment is usually done by giving an overdose of barbiturate anaesthetic into a vein – the cat dies within seconds of the injection being given.
Glomerulonephropathy/ies	Disease affecting the glomerulus and often causing loss of protein from the bloodstream into the urine.
Glomerulus	The small mass of blood vessels encased in the Bowmans capsule of the nephron. Blood in the glomerular capillaries is filtered here to produce urine which passes through the kidney tubules (being modified as it goes) to the renal pelvis.
Haematology	Laboratory test assessing the blood count, numbers and types of white blood cells and platelets. Also referred to as a complete blood count.
History taking	This is the process by which your veterinarian or nurse gathers information on your cat and all of its problems (clinical signs).
Hyper-	Increased e.g. hyperphosphataemia: increased blood phosphate levels.
Hypercalcaemia	Abnormally high blood calcium levels.
Hyperkalaemia	Abnormally high blood potassium levels.
Hypernatraemia	Abnormally high blood sodium levels.
Hyperparathyroidism	See renal secondary hyperparathyroidism.
Hyperphosphataemia	Abnormally high blood phosphate levels.
Hyperthyroidism	A common condition, especially in older cats, where there is an overactive thyroid producing excess amounts of thyroid hormones. The most common clinical signs are weight loss in spite of a good appetite.
Hypo-	Reduced e.g. hypokalaemia: low levels of potassium in the blood; hypoproteinaemia: low levels of protein in the blood.
Hypocalcaemia	Abnormally low blood calcium levels.

Term	Definition
Hypokalaemia	Abnormally low blood potassium levels.
Hyponatraemia	Abnormally low blood sodium levels.
Hypoproteinaemia	Abnormally low blood protein levels.
Inappetence	Poor appetite.
Inflammation	A response of injured or damaged cells which helps to wall off the problem, eliminate infectious substances (for example) and restore healthy tissue. The classic signs of inflammation are: ■ Heat ■ Pain ■ Redness ■ Swelling ■ Loss of function.
Inflammatory	Pertaining to inflammation.
IRIS	The International Renal Interest Society – a panel of internationally respected veterinary nephrologists who have devised recommendations for the assessment and treatment of renal disease in cats and dogs. www.iris-kidney.com.
Nephritis	Inflammatory process present within the kidney/s. This term can be further qualified according to the location of the inflammation – for example: ■ Pyelonephritis: inflammation of the kidney and renal pelvis ■ Chronic interstitial nephritis (CIN): inflammation of the kidney including the tissues between the nephrons. CIN is commonly diagnosed in cats with chronic kidney disease and often represents an end-stage of many different types of kidney disease. ■ Glomerulonephritis: inflammation of the kidney and glomerulus.

Term	Definition
Nephron	The functional unit of the kidney: the nephron is a tubule which produces urine and carries it to the renal pelvis. Each normal feline kidney contains about 200,000 nephrons.
Nephropathy	Abnormal development or disease causing destruction of the kidney.
Nephrosis	Degeneration of the kidney tissue e.g. following exposure to a toxic substance.
Nephrotic syndrome	The term used specifically to describe patients with such severe protein loss from the kidneys that their blood protein levels are sub-normal (hypoproteinaemia) and the cat is suffering from clinical signs as a consequence of this (e.g. ascites: fluid development within the abdomen).
Nephrotoxin/s	Substance/s which is/are toxic to the kidneys. Examples include substances which can be eaten (e.g. lily plants) and medications (e.g. certain antibiotics, non-steroidal anti-inflammatory drugs).
Oedema	The accumulation of excessive amounts of watery fluid in the cells or spaces between the cells. This can lead to puffiness of the skin and is a potential consequence of hypoproteinaemia.
Pathologist	A specialist in pathology who is able to diagnose the cause and/or type of disease by examining biopsy samples. Clinical pathologists also interpret blood and urine tests.
Pathology	The study of disease.
Physical examination	Examination of body systems by a veterinarian or nurse. Typically this includes listening to the chest, opening the mouth and feeling the abdomen.
Physiological	Relating to normal healthy function of body organs.
Pica	An abnormal appetite – for example eating cat litter, soil, licking concrete. Often associated with anaemia in cats.
Pleural fluid	Accumulation of fluid in the chest space around the lungs.
Polydipsia	An increased thirst.
Polyuria	Increased volume of urine produced (usually noticed as the cat is passing normal or larger volumes of urine more frequently).

Term	Definition
Pre-renal	Before the kidney – pertaining to events occurring before the kidney is reached. For example causes of pre-renal azotaemia include dehydration and shock which both reduce the blood flow to the kidneys and hence reduce the ability of the kidneys to excrete protein breakdown products.
Post-renal	After the kidney – pertaining to events occurring after the kidney. For example post-renal proteinuria can be seen as a result of cystitis (inflammation of the bladder).
Prognosis	A forecast of the likely long-term outlook for a cat with a given condition/s.
Proteinuria	Abnormally high levels of protein in the urine (normally there should be very little protein present in the urine). Causes include urinary tract infections, presence of blood, glomerulonephropathy.
Proteinuric	Suffering from proteinuria.
Pyelitis/pyelonephritis	Inflammation of the renal pelvis. In pyelonephritis cases, the inflammation has spread to involve the kidney tissue as well as the pelvis.
Radiograph	X-ray.
Refractometer	An instrument that can measure the concentration of urine.
Renal	Relating to the kidney/s.
Renal pelvis	The location where urine produced by the nephrons accumulates. From here, urine flows via the ureters to the bladder.
Renal secondary hyperparathyroidism	The situation where the parathyroid glands enlarge and produce excessive amounts of parathyroid hormone. Increased blood phosphate levels (hyperphosphataemia) and reduced calcitriol production by the kidneys are the main triggers for the development of this condition. Renal secondary hyperparathyroidism is an important condition since it contributes to the clinical signs of CKD and progression of renal disease.
Sedation	Providing a state of calm and muscle relaxation using drugs. The cat is still conscious but, depending on the drugs used, may appear quite sleepy.

Term	Definition
Specific gravity	Specific gravity is a measure of urine concentration. A refractometer is used to measure the urine specific gravity. Water has a specific gravity of 1.000. Normal cats usually produce urine with a specific gravity of at least 1.040. The lower the specific gravity, the less concentrated the urine is. Kidney disease reduces a cat's ability to produce concentrated urine and the specific gravity falls to less than 1.035. In severe cases of kidney disease, the urine specific gravity can be as low as 1.015. It is important to bear in mind that other illnesses (e.g. diabetes mellitus, hyperthyroidism) can also lower the specific gravity.
Systemic hypertension	An increase in the blood pressure of the systemic blood supply (the blood supply to all of the body except the lungs).
Toxin	Poison. A nephrotoxin is poisonous to the kidneys.
Trauma	Injury or wound.
Uraemic syndrome	This term is used to describe the clinical signs which are seen in cats with chronic kidney disease. Examples would include gastritis (inflammation of the stomach lining causing vomiting and poor appetite), systemic hypertension (high blood pressure) and metabolic acidosis (blood more acidic than it should be).
Urea	One of the protein breakdown products that is normally excreted by the kidneys and hence accumulates in the blood of cats with kidney disease. Blood urea levels are also affected by illnesses other than kidney disease – for example levels increase following a meal and are also high in cats suffering from dehydration.
Ureter	Small tube which takes urine from each kidney to the bladder.
Urethra	Tube which carries urine from the bladder to the outside of the body.
Urinalysis	Laboratory analysis of a urine sample e.g. number of cells, acidity, protein levels, concentration (specific gravity).
Urine protein to creatinine ratio	A laboratory test which quantifies the severity of proteinuria. Ratios greater than 0.4 are currently considered to be abnormally high. Also known as a UPC or PCR test.

Converting SI units to Conventional units and vice versa

Parameter	To convert Conventional to SI multiply by...	To convert SI to Conventional multiply by...
Urea	0.357	2.8
Creatinine	88.4	0.0113
Phosphate	0.323	3.1
Potassium	1	1
Sodium	1	1
Calcium	0.25	4
Albumin	10	0.1
Globulin	10	0.1
Total protein	10	0.1
Bicarbonate	1	1
Packed cell volume (PCV) or haematocrit	0.01	100
Haemoglobin (Hb)	10	0.1

In memory of Morgan